CONTENTS

DOCTOR · WHO

STARSHIPS AND SPACESTATIONS

JUSTIN RICHARDS

BBC
BOOKS

Published by BBC Books, an imprint of Ebury Publishing.

Ebury Publishing is a division of the Random House Group.

10 9 8 7 6 5 4 3 2 1

ISBN 978 1 84607 423 3

Commissioning Editors:	Mathew Clayton and Albert DePetrillo	Design
Project Editor:	Steve Tribe	Cover
Creative Consultant:	Justin Richards	Produc

Printed and bound by Firmengruppe APPL, aprinta druck, Wemding, Germany.

BBC Books would like to thank the following for providing photographs and for permission to reproduce copyright material. While every effort has been made to trace and acknowledge all copyright holders, we would like to apologise should there have been any errors or omissions. All images copyright © BBC, except:

pages 18 and 84 (bottom right) Raymond P. Cusick

page 19 John Wood (composition by Lee Binding)

pages 21 (top), 23, 24, 35 (bottom right), 45 (bottom right), 51, 58 (bottom right), 74 (bottom) and 92 (middle) Mat Irvine

page 59 (top) Steve Cambden

page 78 (middle) George Reed/Steve Cambden, page 78 (bottom) Len Hutton/Steve Cambden

page 79 (top) Richard Conway/Steve Cambden

page 82 (top) Mike Tucker

Artwork of the *Valiant* on pages 10–11 is © and courtesy of Peter McKinstry.

Classic series artwork on pages 16, 21 (bottom), 43, 75, 76 (top), 83 (bottom right), 84 (bottom right), 86 are © and courtesy of Gavin Rymill. All production designs and storyboards are reproduced courtesy of the Doctor Who Art Department.

Image on page 60 (bottom left) is courtesy of Millennium FX.

All computer-generated imagery courtesy of The Mill, including the main images on pages 12, 14 (top), 15 (top), 28, 38–39, 46, 47, 56 (top), 61, 62, 64, 65, 68–69, 72–73, 88 (top) and 94–95.

With additional thanks to:

Will Cohen, Russell T Davies, Neill Gorton, Ian Grutchfield, Clayton Hickman, David J. Howe, Mat Irvine, Peter McKinstry, Marianne Paton, Nicholas Payne, Edward Russell, Gary Russell, Tom Spilsbury, Peter Ware and all at *Doctor Who Magazine*, Edward Thomas, Alex Thompson and Mike Tucker.

STARSHIPS AND SPACESTATIONS

Through the millennia, the Time Lords of Gallifrey observed and catalogued the universe. They rarely intervened in the affairs of other races, preferring to watch rather than to get involved.

Occasionally, however, they did involve themselves in the history of other races and planets. Ironically, it was one of these interventions that led to their destruction. Their decision to send a renegade Time Lord known as the Doctor to prevent the creation of the terrible Daleks led to the Great Time War in which it seemed both races were utterly destroyed.

But before that, the Doctor had disagreed with the Time Lord policy of non-involvement. He argued that there were corners of the universe that had bred the most terrible things – and they had to be fought. Stealing a TARDIS, he left Gallifrey…

It is strange that, in a history of space travel, the Time Lords hardly feature – except in the interventionist form of their renegade champion, the Doctor. The Time Lords soon set themselves up above such mundane technology as simple starships and spacestations.

In the so-called Old Times, many millennia earlier, the founder of Time Lord society, Rassilon, created mighty 'bow ships' to destroy the Great Vampires that were threatening the universe. A Great Vampire could only be killed if its heart was completely destroyed – by a mighty bolt of steel fired from a bow ship.

Occasionally, in their later years, the Time Lords made use of a huge spacestation linked by a temporal 'door' to the Matrix itself – the repository of all Time Lord knowledge and expertise… It was here that they once put the Doctor on trial.

For the most part, though, the Time Lords relied on their TT capsules – their TARDISes.

To describe a TARDIS as a spaceship is like calling a modern jet aircraft a 'chariot'. It might travel from place to place, but the speed and nature of the journey is very different.

Add to that the ability to travel in time, and the Time Lords had spacecraft that were truly unique.

As we chart the development of space travel, mainly from the perspective of that influential planet Earth, the TARDIS must rate as the most advanced of the vehicles we cover.

Yet, despite being so much more than a simple spaceship, it does deserve a mention.

TARDIS, after all, stands for Time And Relative Dimension In Space…

EARTH SPACE PROGRAMMES

While Neil Armstrong's celebrated 'giant leap for Mankind' confirmed NASA in the public memory and imagination as the most famous of the space agencies, it was by no means the only official body sending people into space in the 1960s and into the twenty-first century. The UK's own space programme, formed from the British Rocket Group of the 1950s and 1960s, even sent astronauts to Mars. But the most prestigious organisation was International Space Command, responsible for the *Zeus* programme of the 1980s, and for the Weather Control Moon lunar base in the twenty-first century.

THE ZEUS PROGRAMME

Zeus was overseen from International Space Command's Snowcap Base at the South Pole. Its multinational team, commanded by General Cutler, combined military and scientific expertise. In overall control was General Secretary Wigner, based at ISC Headquarters in Geneva and in constant liaison with the UN's equivalent force, UNIT. Snowcap Base was equipped with Cobra Missiles for self-defence, as well as launch facilities for Demeter Rockets. It also had a Z Bomb – a 'doomsday weapon' capable of splitting the planet in half – designed as a deterrent against world war. Several were positioned at secret strategic positions around the world.

In 1986, when Earth's twin planet Mondas appeared, Snowcap was in control of *Zeus 4* – a mission manned by astronauts Schulz and Williams to investigate cosmic rays. Out of fuel and pulled off course by the arrival of the new planet, *Zeus 4* exploded before a recovery mission – *Zeus 5*, manned by Cutler's son – could reach it. With Mondas draining away Earth's energy, its inhabitants, the Cybermen, sent an expeditionary force to Snowcap. They planned to use the Z Bomb to destroy Earth before Mondas absorbed too much energy. The intervention of the Doctor and his friends helped defeat the Cyber force, which was susceptible to the effects of radiation from the Z Bomb, and Mondas was destroyed.

Story
The Tenth Planet
Written by
Kit Pedler & Gerry Davis
Featuring
the First Doctor,
Ben and Polly
First broadcast
8–29 October 1966
4 episodes

MARS PROBE

Britain's *Mars Probe* missions during the 1970s attracted most attention when disaster struck. After several successful landings, *Mars Probe 7* seemed like another routine expedition to the red planet. For twelve hours, astronauts Frank Michaels and Joe Lefee sent back pictures and reports from the surface of Mars. Then – silence.

Story
The Ambassadors of Death
Written by
David Whitaker
Featuring
**the Third Doctor, UNIT
and Liz**
First broadcast
21 March–2 May 1970
7 episodes

Just as it seemed all hope was gone, *Mars Probe 7* blasted off from Mars to return to Earth. Monitored as usual by Space Control, under the command of Ralph Cornish, astronaut Charles Van Lyden was sent up in *Recovery 7* to dock with the *Mars Probe* capsule and find out what had happened. As Van Lyden entered the capsule, contact was lost and a strange burst of alien sound was broadcast. Working with UNIT, who were in charge of security at Space Control, the Doctor realised that the sound was in fact a message. But before he could answer it, a reply was broadcast from somewhere nearby.

When *Recovery 7* returned to Earth, it was hijacked and the astronauts kidnapped from inside. In fact, these were not the original astronauts at all, but alien ambassadors who were forced to attack government installations and make it seem that the aliens were out for war. Their intentions were actually peaceful, and the culprit turned out to be General Carrington – the head of the newly established Space Security Department. He had encountered the aliens when he was an astronaut on *Mars Probe 6*. They had accidentally killed his fellow astronaut Jim Daniels, not realising their touch could be fatal to humans.

It was up to the Doctor to risk his life by piloting *Recovery 8* to the alien mothership and negotiating for the release of the real astronauts in return for the safety of the ambassadors.

CRAYFORD'S XK5

Britain's space programme continued for many years after the Ambassadors incident, although direct contact with aliens was rather limited. An exception was the XK Project. By the late 1970s, when young journalist Sarah Jane Smith reported on the project, Space Control had been moved to the outskirts of the Cotswold village of Devesham.

Astronaut Guy Crayford was responsible for testing the new XK5 space freighter. While he was out in deep space, the ship vanished from the tracking systems. It was assumed the ship had collided with an asteroid.

In fact, Crayford had been captured by the Kraals, an alien race whose chief scientist, Styggron, convinced Crayford that the Kraals had saved him when his ship suffered gyro failure. Styggron told Crayford that the Kraals needed to escape from their own irradiated planet, Oseidon. They intended to infiltrate human defences using android copies of the Space Defence Station personnel trained in a replica of Devesham. Crayford would return to Earth from – he claimed – an orbit round Jupiter, but bringing the androids with him…

The arrival of the Doctor and Sarah in the replica village eventually led Crayford to realise he had been duped and that the Kraals intended to wipe out the human race with a deadly virus. Crayford confronted Styggron back on the real Earth, and the alien scientist was killed before he could signal to Kraal Marshal Chedaki that it was safe to invade.

Story
The Android Invasion
Written by
Terry Nation
Featuring
the Fourth Doctor, UNIT, Sarah and Harry
First broadcast
22 November– 13 December 1975
4 episodes

PRETENDING TO FLY

Operation Golden Age was a huge con trick played on unsuspecting people who believed they were going to a new world, to start a new life away from the pollution and decay of modern society. The volunteers went into suspended animation, to be woken when they reached the new planet.

In truth, there was no new planet – and no spaceships. Professor Whitaker had discovered a way of rolling back time. Having brought dinosaurs from prehistory into modern London to clear it of people, he intended to take Earth back to what he and his colleagues believed was a golden age before humans evolved. The sleepers from the spaceship would then wake up – on an unspoilt Earth.

With dinosaurs running riot in London, the Doctor managed to discover the truth and unmask a traitor in UNIT's own ranks, foiling Whitaker's plan and telling the horrified spaceship volunteers the truth.

Story
Invasion of the Dinosaurs
Written by
Malcolm Hulke
Featuring
the Third Doctor, UNIT and Sarah
First broadcast
12 January–16 February 1974
6 episodes

THE VALIANT

A huge flying aircraft carrier under the command of UNIT, the *Valiant* was the venue for the first meeting between the human race and the alien Toclafane in the early years of the twenty-first century.

New Prime Minister Harry Saxon claimed to have made contact with these aliens, who wanted only to help the people of Earth. Saxon set up a meeting on the *Valiant* attended by himself and the President of the USA. But it was all a trap. Saxon was in fact the Doctor's old enemy the Master – a renegade Time Lord with a hunger for power and a passion for destruction and mayhem. The Toclafane killed the US President, before billions of them appeared and wiped out one-tenth of the Earth's population.

For a year, the Master ruled with the Toclafane, building a great fleet of rockets with which he planned to conquer other worlds. He held the Doctor and his friends prisoner on board the *Valiant*, which he made his base of operations. To stop the Doctor opposing him, the Master turned

Story
**The Sound of Drums &
Last of the Time Lords**
Written by
Russell T Davies
Featuring
**the Tenth Doctor, Martha
and Captain Jack**
First broadcast
23–30 June 2007
2 episodes

him into an old man – and later into a small wizened creature that looked every bit as old as the Doctor's 900 years…

But the Doctor's friend Martha had escaped from the *Valiant* when the Toclafane attacked. She spent a whole year travelling the Earth and telling stories of the Doctor and how he could save the world if everyone believed in him. In a final showdown on the flight deck of the *Valiant*, the Master's plans were thwarted and the Doctor recovered. With help from Captain Jack Harkness and Martha's family, the Master was defeated and time snapped back onto its true course – a history in which the Toclafane invasion never occurred.

THE ATMOS INCIDENT

While the *Valiant* was usually kept in high-altitude flight, even when being serviced and repaired, it was brought close to ground level during the attempted Sontaran invasion (see p.93).

UNIT called in the *Valiant* so that its huge jet turbine engines could be used to dissipate the toxic gas created by the Atmos System – a key part of the Sontaran plan to take control of Earth and turn it into a Clone World where they could create Sontaran troops for use in their unceasing war against the Rutans.

THE TOCLAFANE

The Master called the aliens he brought to Earth 'the Toclafane', but the Doctor knew that this was a name he had made up.

The Toclafane were technologically advanced spheres, about the size of footballs, speaking in sing-song voices like naughty children. They hovered and flew through the air and could emit energy pulses or use knives and cutting tools that slid out from their casings.

They appeared to be mechanical, but when Martha managed to open a Toclafane sphere she discovered that inside was a withered, disembodied human head plugged into the mechanisms. This was what the human race would become in order to survive in Utopia trillions of years in the future. They had been brought back to the present by the Master to conquer the Earth and rule over their own ancient ancestors.

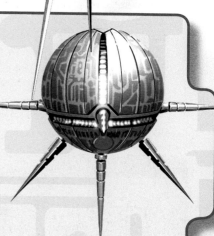

FULLY ROUNDED DESIGN

These design drawings show how the Toclafane spheres open and how they deploy their weaponry. All except one of the Toclafane themselves were computer-generated images created by The Mill.

FINGERS DEPLOYED

ATTACK MODE

MAKING THE VALIANT FLY

The **Doctor Who** Art Department, under the supervision of overall Production Designer Edward Thomas, drew up plans and paintings of what the *Valiant* should look like. These were derived from and inspired by the description in the script for *The Sound of Drums* by Russell T Davies.

These designs and ideas were then passed to the digital effects designers at The Mill who created the final *Valiant* as a completely computer-generated image. The exception of course was the interior of the *Valiant*. The main flight deck was an enormous set constructed by the Art Department at the **Doctor Who** studios outside Cardiff, while the lower levels and service areas were created on location.

The images on this page show some of the original designs for the interior and the exterior of the *Valiant*.

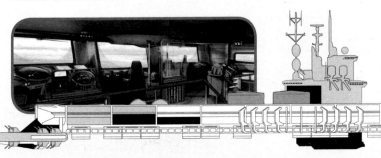

Top and upper left: Design paintings of the *Valiant*'s impressive interior. Bottom left: A design schematic of the *Valiant*.

THE MASTER'S WAR FLEET

Once he had conquered the Earth with help from his Toclafane allies, the Master set about building a fleet of war rockets to conquer other worlds and create a new Time Lord empire.

Russia was designated Shipyard Number One. From the Black Sea to the Bering Straits, the land was covered with rockets – a hundred thousand of them, with engines powered by black hole converters created in the Fusion Mills of China, ready to wage war against the universe. Other, smaller shipyards were constructed all across what was left of the world – another hundred thousand rockets, ready to take the fight into Braccatolian space and start an empire that would last for a hundred trillion years.

But Martha used the countdown to launch as a countdown for another purpose. As it reached zero, everyone she had ever spoken to – everyone to whom they had in turn passed on the message – thought of the Doctor. The power of these simultaneous thoughts, focused by the Archangel network of telepathic satellites the Master had set up to exert his own mental control over the world, was enough to restore the Doctor to health and defeat the Master's plans.

When Captain Jack Harkness destroyed the Master's Paradox Machine, which had enabled the Toclafane to return to their own past, history snapped back into its proper shape. The Master's rule was cancelled out – it never happened. And equally, his mighty war fleet was never created...

SCRIPT EXTRACT
THE ANCIENT DOCTOR

FX: THE CGI DOCTOR appears.
Head only, on a thin neck.
Blinking, dazed, he is tiny,
ancient, 1 ft high, with a
lined, parched face, big eyes,
though slitted by the weight
of 900 y/o eyelids. Mewling.

Left: An initial design painting of how the ancient form of the Doctor might look.
Right: The finished computer generated image, created using measurements and data from David Tennant's own face so the CGI could copy his actual expressions.

CREATING AN EFFECT

When Martha gazed out over the vast shipyard of rockets in *Last of the Time Lords*, actress Freema Agyeman was looking at… nothing. No rockets, no flying Toclafane spheres, no launch facilities.

The whole of the rocket shipyard was created as a computer image, with the characters of Martha and Tom – and later the Doctor and the Master – added into it.

The Toclafane themselves were also created as digital, computer-generated images, though one actual sphere was also built for close-ups and certain other shots.

The head that Martha and her friends find inside the Toclafane sphere when they open it up was created by prosthetics company Millennium Effects – which was also responsible for making actor David Tennant look like an old version of the Doctor in this story.

The ancient, wizened creature that the Doctor becomes when the Master ages him still further was again a computer-generated image (or CGI), created by expert animators at The Mill and added into the scenes of the episode after they had been shot weeks earlier.

SCRIPT EXTRACT
ROCKETS

FX: Digital Matte Painting of
ROCKET SHIPYARD, a huge vista,
hundreds of them, stretching
away to the horizon. Big, crude,
traditional rockets, spires
pointing skywards.

Left: Martha and Tom look down on the empty space where The Mill will add the Master's rocket shipyard.

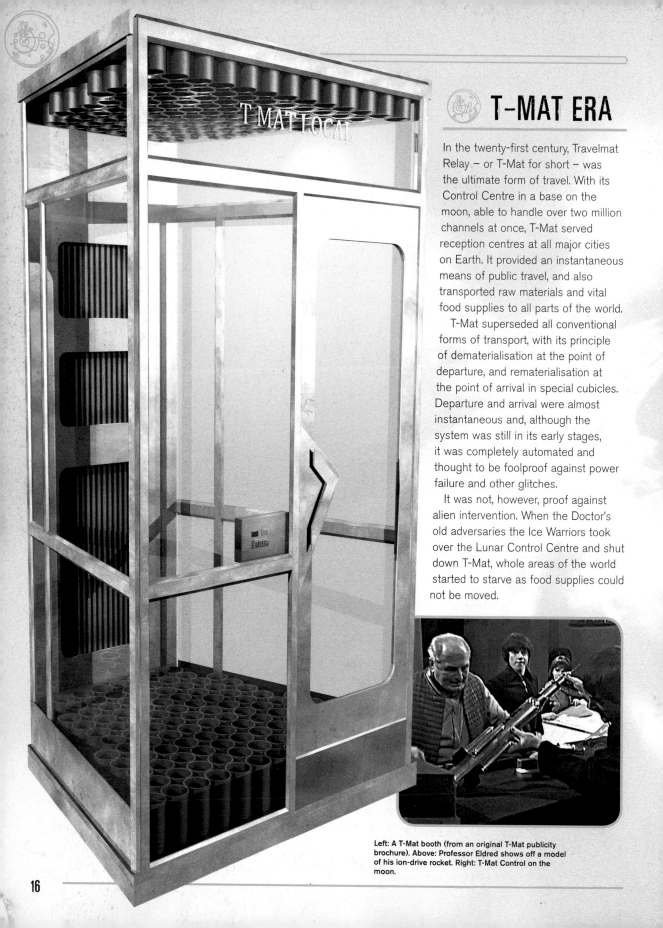

T-MAT ERA

In the twenty-first century, Travelmat Relay – or T-Mat for short – was the ultimate form of travel. With its Control Centre in a base on the moon, able to handle over two million channels at once, T-Mat served reception centres at all major cities on Earth. It provided an instantaneous means of public travel, and also transported raw materials and vital food supplies to all parts of the world.

T-Mat superseded all conventional forms of transport, with its principle of dematerialisation at the point of departure, and rematerialisation at the point of arrival in special cubicles. Departure and arrival were almost instantaneous and, although the system was still in its early stages, it was completely automated and thought to be foolproof against power failure and other glitches.

It was not, however, proof against alien intervention. When the Doctor's old adversaries the Ice Warriors took over the Lunar Control Centre and shut down T-Mat, whole areas of the world started to starve as food supplies could not be moved.

Left: A T-Mat booth (from an original T-Mat publicity brochure). Above: Professor Eldred shows off a model of his ion-drive rocket. Right: T-Mat Control on the moon.

But worse was to follow. The Ice Warriors sent Martian seed pods to various cities around the globe, and the fungus that grew from these began to spread rapidly and deplete the air of oxygen.

Luckily, despite Earth's short-sighted total reliance on T-Mat, the Doctor was able to enlist the help of Professor Eldred, an ageing space engineer who had managed to build his own ion-jet rocket. The Doctor, Jamie and Zoe used the rocket to get to the moon, where they were eventually able to defeat the Ice Warriors. The invasion fleet and the deadly alien fungus were destroyed.

The Earth authorities had learned from the mistake of relying on T-Mat to the exclusion of other methods of transport. With Earth's population also increasing rapidly, it was becoming clear that conventional space travel was essential to the survival of the human race – and the establishment of an expanding Earth Empire…

Story
The Seeds of Death
Written by
Brian Hayles
Featuring
the Second Doctor,
Jamie and Zoe
First broadcast
25 January–1 March 1969
6 episodes

THE EARTH EMPIRE

After the T-Mat interlude, humanity soon returned to the exploration of space. Before long, the Solar System had been explored and mankind was sending probes and survey ships deeper and deeper into space.

As Earth's population grew and living conditions on the planet deteriorated, there was an increasing interest in colonising other worlds. As Earth slowly but surely established its empire in space, there were two main driving forces behind space exploration – the attraction of the new frontier, as star pioneers sought out new planets and places to live, and the need for materials and supplies to keep Earth itself going.

> Story
> **The Space Pirates**
> Written by
> **Robert Holmes**
> Featuring
> **the Second Doctor, Jamie
> and Zoe**
> First broadcast
> **8 March–12 April 1969**
> **6 episodes**

POLICING THE SPACEWAYS

Policing the Empire was a huge task. The authorities relied on ever-advancing technology to try to keep the mining conglomerates and the lone prospectors in check, as well as protecting and policing the pioneers.

Space beacons guided ships, as lighthouses once had. But space beacons, like lighthouses, could be interfered with to lure unsuspecting ships to a terrible fate at the hands of smugglers and pirates.

Even with their huge V-Ships and the fast, short-range 'Minnows', the agents of Earth Space Corps struggled to keep order.

PIONEERS AND COLONISTS

Leaving Earth in the early days of the Empire was a risky undertaking. Many colony ships never reached their destinations, and even routine flights could be dangerous. A flight to the Astra colony in 2493 crashed on the remote planet Dido. This was catastrophic for the ship's passengers and the native population – all killed in an explosion engineered by a murderer trying to evade justice. Ultimately, the only human survivor was Vicki, a girl who was rescued by the Doctor and travelled with him in the TARDIS for a while.

> Story
> **The Rescue**
> Written by
> **David Whitaker**
> Featuring
> **the First Doctor, Barbara,
> Ian and Vicki**
> First broadcast
> **2–9 January 1965**
> **2 episodes**

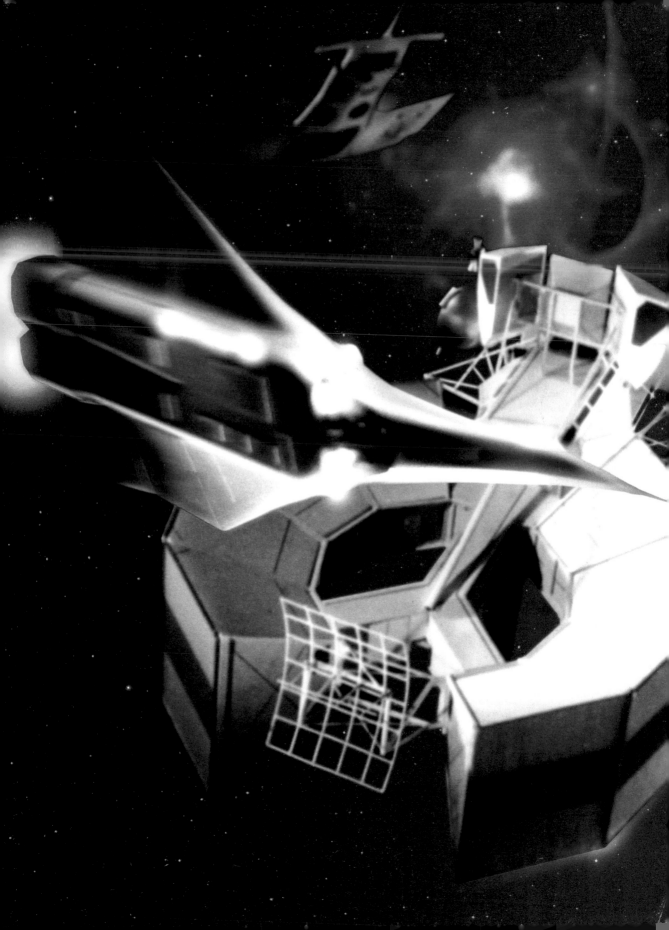

THE MINING CONGLOMERATES

By the late twenty-fifth century, the hold of the mining combines and conglomerates was tightening. Earth was overcrowded and desperately needed mineral supplies to build living units on vast floating islands above the planet, each housing 500 million people. This provided an excuse for companies like the Interplanetary Mining Corporation to maximise their profits. IMC operations on the planet Uxarieus demonstrated this. Though Uxarieus had been designated as suitable for colonisation, Captain Dent of IMC Ship 157 (Survey Ship 43) discovered the planet was rich in the mineral duralinium, and tried to evict the colonists – whose dilapidated ship was unlikely to survive take-off.

The colonists were not scared off by savage monsters faked by the IMC team, so Dent resorted to more direct methods. He was stopped first by the intervention of the Doctor and his companion Jo Grant, and then by the arrival of Adjudicator Jurgens from the Bureau of Interplanetary Affairs. Jurgens was in fact the Doctor's old adversary the Master, and his spaceship was a disguised TARDIS. He had discovered from stolen Time Lord datafiles that Uxarieus was home to an immensely powerful 'doomsday' weapon guarded by the primitive descendents of an advanced alien race. Only the Doctor was able to see off the threat from IMC and prevent the Master from getting hold of the weapon.

More evidence of the lengths the mining companies and prospectors would go to was provided by the events on the Sense-Sphere, where a group of prospectors searching for molybdenum poisoned the water supply of the native Sensorites with deadly nightshade. When the Doctor and his companions arrived on an Earth ship held captive above the Sense-Sphere by the generally peaceful Sensorites, the situation was resolved. By then the large companies had turned their attention to another planet in the vicinity – the Ood-Sphere (see p.31).

Story
Colony in Space
Written by
Malcolm Hulke
Featuring
the Third Doctor
and Jo
First broadcast
10 April–15 May 1971
6 episodes

Story
The Sensorites
Written by
Peter R Newman
Featuring
the First Doctor, Susan,
Barbara and Ian
First broadcast
20 June–1 August 1964
6 episodes

LUXURY LINERS

For those fortunate enough to be able to get away from Earth, this was also a time of great adventure and prosperity. Amongst the rugged cargo vessels and the mining ships, great luxury liners made the trips between an increasing number of populated planets.

As early as the twenty-second century, the *Empress* was ferrying passengers between Station 9 and the planet Azure. On one fateful journey, the *Empress* came out of warp halfway through the scientific survey ship *Hecate*, and the two ships were locked together in space. The Doctor arrived with Romana and K-9 to find dangerous dimensional instabilities, as well as monstrous Mandrels on the loose. These creatures were a rich source of the dangerous – and illegal – addictive drug vraxoin and were being smuggled from their home planet, Eden, by an unscrupulous scientist called Tryst, who had captured them on data crystals inside a Continuous Event Transmuter. The Doctor unlocked the two ships and trapped Tryst inside his own transmuter machine.

Story
Nightmare of Eden
Written by
Bob Baker
Featuring
the Fourth Doctor,
Romana and K-9
First broadcast
24 November–15
December 1979
4 episodes

By the late thirtieth century, space travel for pleasure had become even more luxurious. Ships were still occasionally prey to pirates and other criminals – and the security officer on the ill-fated *Hyperion III* even planned to rob his own ship of the valuable ore it was carrying from the planet Mogar. To add to the troubles of Commodore 'Tonker' Travers, amongst the passengers was Professor Lasky – an agronomist taking rare plant pods from Mogar to Earth. The pods 'hatched' after an accident, and deadly plant creatures called Vervoids set about killing the passengers and crew. The Doctor and his friend Mel were able to destroy the Vervoids and foil the plans of Security Officer Rudge and his Mogarian associates.

Story
The Trial of a Time Lord
– Terror of the Vervoids
Written by
Pip and Jane Baker
Featuring
the Sixth Doctor and Mel
First broadcast
1–22 November 1986
4 episodes

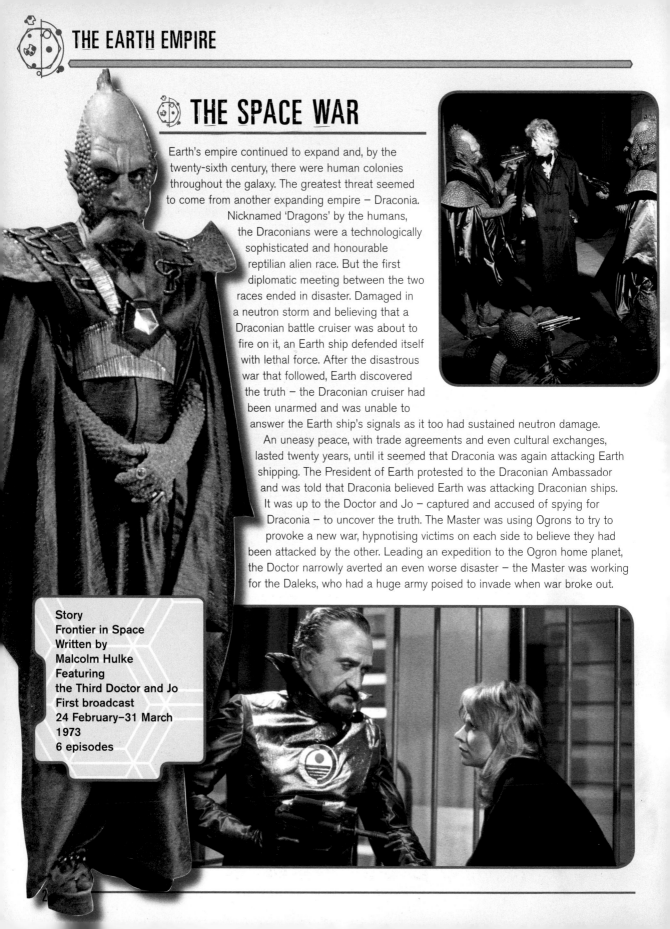

THE SPACE WAR

Earth's empire continued to expand and, by the twenty-sixth century, there were human colonies throughout the galaxy. The greatest threat seemed to come from another expanding empire – Draconia. Nicknamed 'Dragons' by the humans, the Draconians were a technologically sophisticated and honourable reptilian alien race. But the first diplomatic meeting between the two races ended in disaster. Damaged in a neutron storm and believing that a Draconian battle cruiser was about to fire on it, an Earth ship defended itself with lethal force. After the disastrous war that followed, Earth discovered the truth – the Draconian cruiser had been unarmed and was unable to answer the Earth ship's signals as it too had sustained neutron damage.

An uneasy peace, with trade agreements and even cultural exchanges, lasted twenty years, until it seemed that Draconia was again attacking Earth shipping. The President of Earth protested to the Draconian Ambassador and was told that Draconia believed Earth was attacking Draconian ships. It was up to the Doctor and Jo – captured and accused of spying for Draconia – to uncover the truth. The Master was using Ogrons to try to provoke a new war, hypnotising victims on each side to believe they had been attacked by the other. Leading an expedition to the Ogron home planet, the Doctor narrowly averted an even worse disaster – the Master was working for the Daleks, who had a huge army poised to invade when war broke out.

Story
Frontier in Space
Written by
Malcolm Hulke
Featuring
the Third Doctor and Jo
First broadcast
24 February–31 March 1973
6 episodes

MODELLING THE FUTURE

Shown here are some of the impressive model spaceships used in the making of *Frontier in Space*. Before computer-generated images, all **Doctor Who**'s space scenes were created using detailed models hung from wires or (in later years) shot against a blue or green background that was then replaced with a starscape using an electronic process known as Colour Separation Overlay (a similar technique to today's 'green-screen' process).

So that the wires were less obvious to the viewer, both the models and the camera were sometimes upside-down. When the film is shown the right way up, the wires are therefore below the model.

The models for *Frontier in Space* were designed and built by one of the most senior visual effects designers in the business, Bernard Wilkie, with his assistant Ian Scoones.

ILLEGAL TRADING

As well as the petty smuggling that inevitably went on as the spaceways opened and expanded, there were other, more serious breaches of the law. A particularly unpleasant practice was the illegal capture and trade of other sentient races – slave trading.

The Tharils, time-sensitive creatures that could ride the Time Winds between our own universe and the smaller Exo-Space time continuum – were easy prey after the decline of their own empire. They had enslaved lesser races themselves, but their subjects had rebelled – sending vicious Gundan Robots to attack the Tharils at a great feast held in their stronghold at the Gateway between the universes.

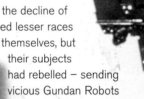

Captain Rorvik was an especially brutal slaver, carrying Tharils in his *Privateer* – a ship built from incredibly dense alloy fused from the material of a collapsed dwarf star, the only material that could hold the Tharils captive. When the ship was ambushed by an Antonine Killer, it crashed at the zero-point between universes close to the Gateway.

After witnessing replays of the downfall of the Tharil Empire, the Doctor and his companions helped the Tharils to escape to freedom. Romana and K-9 – damaged by the Time Winds – went with them. Rorvik, ignoring the Doctor's warnings, attempted to escape by blasting the Gateway with the *Privateer*'s engines. But the mirrors the Tharils used to traverse the universes reflected the energy, and the *Privateer* was destroyed by the back-blast backlash.

Story
Warriors' Gate
Written by
Stephen Gallagher
Featuring
the Fourth Doctor,
Romana, Adric and K-9
First broadcast
3–24 January 1981
4 episodes

MODEL PRIVATEERING
These pictures show some of the model effects for this story – in particular the destruction of the Gateway and the *Privateer*.

⊕ SPACE SAFETY

By the forty-second century, long-range space travel had become routine. Cargo vessels travelled the trade routes rather as the old cargo ships had carried goods across the oceans centuries earlier on Earth. With the growth in the number of trading companies, and with many ships owned by private contractors or consortia, regulating the spaceways became increasingly difficult.

A case study in the dangers of ignoring safety regulations was 'the *Pentallian* Incident'. Operating in the Torajii System, the *Pentallian* was a cargo vessel under the command of Kath McDonnell. Working under extreme conditions and pushed to the brink of fatigue, McDonnell used an illegal fusion scoop to take solar energy from a nearby star.

This star was no ordinary sun, but a living creature. The creature possessed several of the crew, and the ship was plunging into the sun when the Doctor arrived. With the help of Martha Jones, the Doctor was able to restart the engines and jettison the illegal – sentient – fuel. The ship continued on its way, but with the loss of several crew members, including Captain McDonnell and her husband…

Story
42
Written by
Chris Chibnall
Featuring
the Tenth Doctor
and Martha
First broadcast
19 May 2007
1 episode

CREATING THE PENTALLIAN

Like the other spaceships in **Doctor Who**, the *Pentallian* didn't really exist. In fact, like many of the spaceships that have appeared in **Doctor Who** in the twenty-first century, there was not even a physical model of the exterior of the ship.

In the classic series, spaceships were almost always built as miniatures which could be shot against starscapes or model sets, or perhaps added to other backgrounds using video technology. The *Pentallian* only ever existed inside the computers of The Mill – as a computer-generated image (CGI).

The interior of the *Pentallian* was created on location and in the studio. Locations that appear to be very close together might actually be miles apart, and a character who walks from one section of the ship to another might really be performing the role on location several weeks before they then arrive – moments later, it seems – in the studio.

On these pages, you can see some of the design drawings for the interior and the exterior of the ship, as well as images showing how the ship finally appeared in the episode *42*.

PENTALLIAN DRIVE

The ship in *42* was originally called 'Icarus' – named after a character in ancient Greek mythology. Daedalus and his son Icarus made themselves feathered wings to escape from the Labyrinth of King Minos. But, showing off, Icarus ignored his father's warnings and flew too close to the sun. The wax holding the feathers to their frame melted, and his wings came off. Icarus fell to his death in the sea – and into millennia of literature and paintings…

As *42* was being made, the **Doctor Who** production team learned that a spaceship called *Icarus* was appearing in a film due for release about the same time as the episode would be broadcast. So they changed the name to *Pentallian* – naming the ship after the 'Pentalion Drive', a transmat component mentioned in a 1975 **Doctor Who** story, *Revenge of the Cybermen*. Perhaps both the ship and the component are named after one person (albeit with slightly different spellings).

Story
**The Impossible Planet &
The Satan Pit**
Written by
Matt Jones
Featuring
the Tenth Doctor and Rose
First broadcast
**3–10 June 2006
2 episodes**

REACHING THE FINAL FRONTIER

It was not only space travel that became routine. The technology was standardised and became modular. Ships and bases were built to similar basic designs using the same components. The standard Sanctuary Base, for example, was designed to withstand the harshest conditions on alien planets. Though even this rugged design was put to the test with Sanctuary Base 6…

Transported in sections that were then snapped together, the base was set up on a planet orbiting a black hole designated K 37 Gem 5 – an impossible planet. So a team was sent to investigate why the planet was not sucked into the black hole, and to recover the incredibly powerful alien energy source needed to maintain its orbit.

The planet where Santuary Base 6 was erected now has no name. But in the scriptures

of the Veltino it is called Krop Tor – which means 'the bitter pill'. According to legend, they believed that the black hole was itself a demon who had been tricked into devouring the planet, only to spit it out because it was poison.

The truth, as the Doctor and Rose were to discover when they arrived on Sanctuary Base 6, was stranger and deadly dangerous. Deep beneath the planet's surface, the Beast was imprisoned. It felt the humans and their Ood servants in the base above, and reached out to them. Through its own words, recorded in ancient runic symbols, it possessed the telepathic Ood and human archaeologist Toby Zed. Leaving its mindless body still imprisoned, the Beast planned to escape hidden inside Toby's mind.

The Beast was destroyed when the Doctor managed to shut down the energy source that kept the planet safe. Toby was ejected into space to plunge into the heart of the black hole…

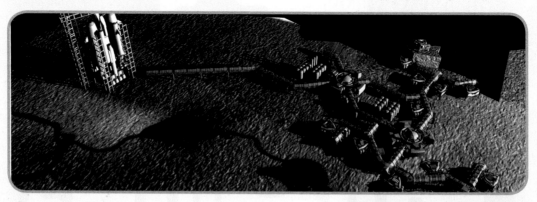

BUILDING THE FRONTIER

While Sanctuary Base 6 seemed like a single, modular set of buildings constructed to a formalised design, it was in fact several places. Parts of the base were constructed as sets in the BBC Wales studios, while others were realised on location.

The **Doctor Who** Art Department created a setting that seemed both futuristic and lived-in – a working environment that contrasted with the ancient ruins in the chambers deep below the planet's surface where the Beast was held prisoner.

The exterior of the base – and the shuttle rocket – were computer-generated images created by The Mill, who also created the enormous Beast itself.

The artwork and photographs on this page show the original designs and the final impressive realisation of Sanctuary Base 6.

OOD OPERATIONS

As well as their human crews, the Sanctuary Bases of the forty-second century had a complement of fifty Ood to serve the main crew. The Ood were a hive-minded race, that communicated with each other using low-level telepathy, and with their human masters using spherical interface devices wired into their heads.

The Ood believed they existed to serve, and were traded as commodities by Ood Operations, a company run by Chief Executive Halpen, based on the Ood home planet – the Ood-Sphere. Ood were used by companies and individuals for everything from space maintenance tasks to domestic help. It seemed there was no task they were unwilling to perform.

Not all humans believed the Ood should serve as – effectively – slaves. The campaign for Ood freedom led by the pressure group Friends of the Ood seemed doomed to failure since the Ood themselves showed no signs of wanting to be free. But all that was to change with the spread of a mysterious infection that seemed to turn affected Ood hostile and murderous – Red Eye…

THE OOD.
THEY CAME FROM A DI
WORLD.
THEY VOYAGE
ONE PURPOSE…
TO SERVE!
BUY ONE NOW – ONL
50 CREDITS

ood operations

CATCHING THE RED EYE

The truth about Red Eye, and about the Ood themselves, was only revealed when the Friends of the Ood finally succeeded in infiltrating and sabotaging Ood Operations on the Ood-Sphere.

After 200 years of trading in Ood, and with the market almost saturated, the price of Ood fell to just 50 credits for the first time. Chief Executive Halpen was under pressure to increase sales, and he personally supervised a sales promotion meeting on the Ood-Sphere. But events were moving at a fast pace, and a secret Halpen thought was hidden for ever was about to be exposed…

When the Doctor and Donna arrived on the Ood-Sphere, the Red Eye was taking hold, and more and more Ood were turning hostile. But the Doctor realised

Story
Planet of the Ood
Written by
Keith Temple
Featuring
the Tenth Doctor and
Donna
First broadcast
19 April 2008
1 episode

the true cause of the problem. He examined 'raw' Ood before they were prepared for sale and found that, instead of the interface device for communication, the Ood naturally have a second brain – a hind-brain – which they hold in their hands. Ood Operations removed this before selling the Ood – in effect mentally crippling the creatures and making them willing slaves. The Ood wish to serve was not natural at all…

Realising that a creature with a separate forebrain and hind-brain could not survive unless there was a third component in their make-up, the Doctor discovered Halpen's secret – an enormous brain which connected all the Ood together in telepathic harmony. Or rather, it once had – until Halpen's forebears had found it beneath the northern glacier on the Ood-Sphere, and set up a psychic barrier to break the connection between the Brain and the Ood.

But the Friends of the Ood had managed to lower the barrier enough for the Brain to start communicating – causing the Red Eye plague. The Doctor and Donna were able to stop Halpen from finally destroying the Brain. Halpen himself had been secretly fed Ood-graft by his servant Ood Sigma, and finally mutated into an Ood.

Freed from their docile slavery, Oodkind were once more connected to their main Brain and to each other. Free at last – to make their own choices, and to sing.

BRAINS BEHIND THE OOD

The impressive and distinctive masks for the Ood themselves had already been created by Neill Gorton's Millennium FX company for *The Impossible Planet*. Now, for *Planet of the Ood*, the **Doctor Who** Art Department had to create not just an isolated base, but a whole planet – not to mention a giant Ood Brain.

On this page you can see some of the original design artwork for the Ood Operations installation (below) and the massive Ood brain (above) together with other concept artwork.

SPACE DOCTORS

Often forgotten in the story of Earth's expansion into space is the increasingly important role played by the medical profession. Particularly during the so-called 'Great Breakout' of *c.*5000 AD, when humanity ventured further and faster out into space.

Even within the solar system, hospital facilities like the Bi-Al Foundation, located on Asteroid K4067, provided medical facilities for space pioneers and for the crews of staging posts like the Titan Base facility.

It was with the expertise and technology of the Bi-Al Foundation, and in particular the help of Professor Marius and his robot dog K-9, that the Doctor was able to counteract the threat of an intelligent alien virus swarm. The virus entered its victims through the optic nerve and took root in the brain, thriving on mental activity.

Story
The Invisible Enemy
Written by
Bob Baker & Dave Martin
Featuring
**the Fourth Doctor,
Leela and K-9**
First broadcast
**1–22 October 1977
4 episodes**

CLOCKWORK MAINTENANCE

Story
The Girl in the Fireplace
Written by
Steven Moffat
Featuring
the Tenth Doctor, Rose and Mickey
First broadcast
6 May 2006
1 episode

Effective and reliable spacecraft maintenance was essential if more accidents and tragedies were to be avoided. One novel solution pioneered aboard some fifty-first-century vessels was the use of repair androids operated by clockwork. With no external power requirements, the androids could operate independently of their ship, activating if and when disaster struck.

Even so, there were unforeseen problems. In the case of the SS *Madame de Pompadour*, a fault in the androids' programming led to disaster aboard the stricken vessel after it was damaged in an ion storm.

Programmed to make use of any compatible technology in order to repair the ship, the clockwork androids killed the human crew and made use of their components. A human eye replaced a surveillance camera; a human heart was used as a fluid pump…

In an effort to repair the ship's main computer, the androids reasoned that the brain of the real Madame de Pompadour when she was 37 (exactly the same age as the ship) would serve as a replacement. They opened time windows to eighteenth-century France to track down Reinette, later to become Madame de Pompadour. Dressed in contemporary clothing and wearing ornate face masks to hide their true nature, the androids attacked the Palace of Versailles to get Reinette's head.

The androids' plans were thwarted by the intervention of the Doctor, who closed the time windows and cut them off from their ship for ever. Realising they had failed, the androids deactivated.

CONTRASTING DESIGNS

The Girl in the Fireplace presents viewers with two very distinct sets of designs. There is the futuristic and functional spaceship, and the lavish and luxurious France of the eighteenth century. Throwing the two worlds together creates a unique set of images, the like of which you could only find in **Doctor Who**.

From a design point of view, the marriage of the two worlds was straightforward. While some of the rooms in Versailles were actually shot on location, others were realised as studio sets. With a ballroom set built right next to one of the spaceship corridors, Reinette and the Doctor can step through from historic France to the space-travelling future.

SATELLITE FIVE

Story
The Long Game
Written by
Russell T Davies
Featuring
**the Ninth Doctor,
Rose and Adam**
First broadcast
**7 May 2005
1 episode**

By the year 200,000, the Fourth Great and Bountiful Human Empire had been established. Earth itself was covered with mega-cities, had five moons and a population of 96 billion, and was the hub of a galactic domain stretching across a million planets and a million species.

Orbiting the Earth, Satellite Five broadcast 600 TV news channels. Journalists gathered, wrote, packaged and sold the news – nothing happened in the Human Empire without it going through Satellite Five. Floor 500 was the Editorial level – where the management was based, and where everyone else aspired to be promoted. The walls were rumoured to be made of gold… In reality, it was very different – cold, abandoned and dilapidated. Satellite Five had been taken over by the Mighty Jagrafess of the Holy Hadrojassic Maxarodenfoe – an expanse of living material, with a sharp-toothed mouth. Manipulating the news enabled the creation of a climate of fear, and subliminal messaging could subvert the economy or change a vote…

The Editor of Satellite Five represented a consortium of banks and worked directly for the Jagrafess. He used human corpses – animated by implanted computer chips that enabled the staff to communicate directly with the news-feed systems – to operate the main control room. The Jagrafess was exposed and destroyed after the intervention of the Ninth Doctor, but even he didn't realise that, behind the Jagrafess, an age-old enemy had been playing a very long game…

GAME STATION

Story
**Bad Wolf &
The Parting of the Ways**
Written by
Russell T Davies
Featuring
**the Ninth Doctor, Rose and
Captain Jack**
**First broadcast
11–18 June 2005
2 episodes**

A century after the destruction of the Jagrafess, Satellite Five had become the Game Station. Run by the Bad Wolf Corporation, it now broadcast not news reports but game shows and reality TV to the enormous population of Earth.

Contestants in the shows were teleported from Earth – anyone could be chosen at any time. The shows included a version of *Big Brother* on Channel 44,000 – with housemates killed rather than evicted – and a version of *The Weakest Link* hosted by a lethal robot called the Anne Droid.

Behind the scenes, the whole operation was run by the Controller, a human woman, linked to the transmissions from the Game Station – the entire output going through her brain. She was installed in the systems at the age of five, so this was the only life she had known. She also knew that lurking in the shadows of space, manipulating every game and harvesting the losing contestants, were the Daleks. They were hiding their own transmissions within the Game Station signals, preparing to attack Earth with a huge fleet created by the Emperor Dalek, who had managed to survive the Great Time War.

It was Rose Tyler – infected with the energy of the Time Vortex – who finally destroyed the Daleks. The Doctor managed to draw the energy out of her and save Rose, but at terrible cost to himself – he was forced to regenerate into his tenth incarnation…

BEHIND THE HEADLINES

Satellite Five was another computer-generated image created by The Mill, from initial designs by the **Doctor Who** Art Department. On this page you can see some of those initial designs and paintings, which are very close to the final computer-generated images created by The Mill.

THE END OF THE EMPIRE

Story
The Mutants
Written by
Bob Baker & Dave Martin
Featuring
the Third Doctor and Jo
First broadcast
8 April–13 May 1972
6 episodes

Empires rise and empires decline and fall. The Earth Empire went through several phases of decline throughout its history. The situation on the planet Solos serves as a definitive example of Earth's change from benevolent autocracy to colonial tyrant, finally ending in failure and abandonment…

Solos was under Earth jurisdiction for 500 years before it finally seceded from the Empire. Much of the population had been pressed into working in the thaesium mines, providing vital ore for the Empire. Some accepted the 'Overlords' from Earth, but others were vehemently opposed to the humans who ruled from their remote Skybase in orbit about the planet. Towards the end of Earth rule, the land of Solos became poisoned, its air unbreathable to humans. The Solonians themselves were mutating into hideous insectoid creatures, which the humans called 'Mutts'. It seemed that the planet was dying, and many of the Solonians blamed experiments conducted by the Marshal, who took control after the assassination of the Earth Administrator. The Marshal was actually behind the murder, knowing that Earth was about to grant Solos independence as the Empire retrenched.

The Marshal's attempts to make the atmosphere breathable for humans, but poisonous to the native population, had accelerated a process that was entirely natural. The seasonal cycle of Solos was drawn out far longer than on other planets, and the Mutants were simply a stage between the humanoid Solonians and advanced creatures with great mental powers. The Doctor reversed the effects of the Marshal's experiment, hastening the mutation to its final evolutionary form before Solos was granted independence.

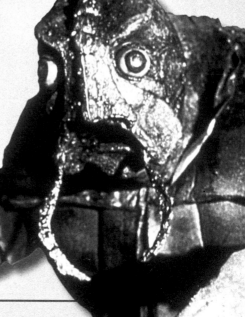

ESCAPING THE END

Despite being the centre of a mighty empire, Earth has been abandoned by its human population several times. Ten million years from now, in the 57th Segment of Time, the population escaped in miniaturised form aboard a giant space 'Ark' headed for the planet Refusis II – a journey that would take 700 years.

FINAL ESCAPE?

The Ark was crewed by the human Guardians of the Human Race, and their servants – the one-eyed Monoids, who had come to Earth when their own planet was dying. They offered their services in return for a place on the Ark. The Monoids were tall, green and reptilian in appearance, with one eye and no mouth. They used special electronic voice boxes to communicate.

The Ark itself contained a jungle, in which live animals, including Indian elephants, monitor lizards, chameleons and locusts, were preserved. Despite a revolt by the Monoids, and a deadly plague mutated from Dodo's common cold, the Ark finally reached its destination and was welcomed by the formless Refusians.

But although the crew of the Ark watched what they thought was the final demise of Earth plunging into the sun, the planet was in fact preserved by the National Trust. Over the billions of years following, it was restored to a 'classic' continental configuration before finally being destroyed by the expanding sun in 5.5/Apple/26 (the year five billion).

Story
The Ark
Written by
**Paul Erickson
& Lesley Scott**
Featuring
**the First Doctor, Steven
and Dodo**
First broadcast
5–26 March 1966
4 episodes

PROJECT NERVA

Long before the pioneers of the Ark abandoned Earth, another Ark in Space was established to enable humankind to cheat the end of the world and outsit eternity.

In the thirtieth century, with deadly solar flares predicted, much of the population went into thermic shelters, knowing that they would die in the firestorms. But some left Earth to become star pioneers – heading out to Andromeda and other colonies.

A small group of specially selected people was put into cryogenic suspension aboard a converted space beacon – Station *Nerva* – to be awakened once the flares had receded. They could then return to Earth and repopulate it, bringing with them stored animal and botanic specimens.

But when the Doctor arrived in the far future, he discovered the 'Ark' (as it was nicknamed) had been attacked by a Wirrn Queen and the systems shut down. The humans had never reawakened, and now the Wirrn were poised to take control.

Fleeing from the humans in Andromeda who had destroyed their breeding grounds, the insectoid Wirrn could live for years in space without fresh oxygen, their lungs recycling the wastes and using enzymes to convert carbon dioxide back into oxygen.

Absorbing the knowledge – and sometimes personalities – of the human sleepers, the Wirrn planned to equip themselves with the knowledge and experience of humanity. But the Doctor was able to hold them off, and the sleepers awoke to return by transmat to Earth.

Story
The Ark in Space
Written by
Robert Holmes
Featuring
the Fourth Doctor, Sarah and Harry
First broadcast
25 January–15 February 1975
4 episodes

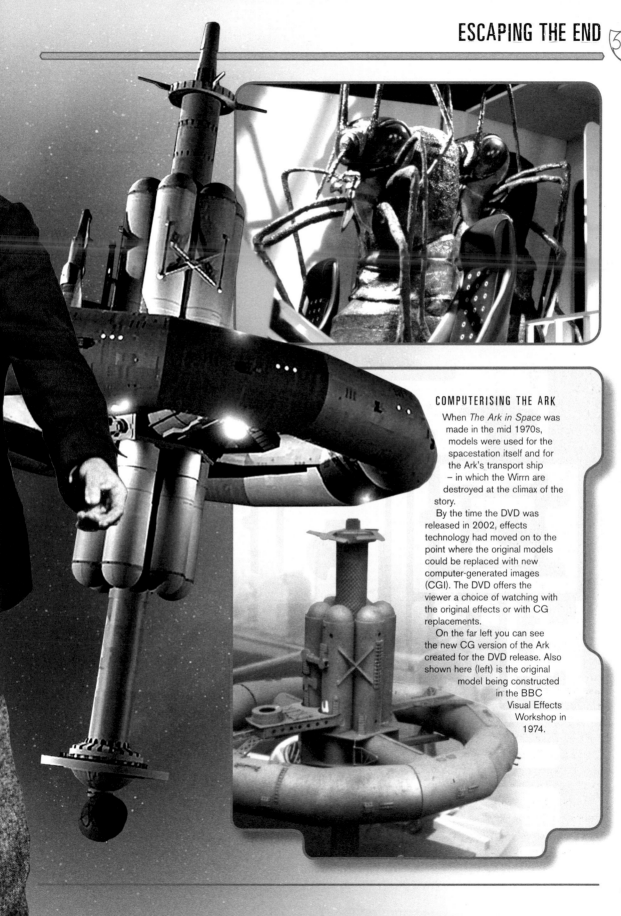

COMPUTERISING THE ARK

When *The Ark in Space* was made in the mid 1970s, models were used for the spacestation itself and for the Ark's transport ship – in which the Wirrn are destroyed at the climax of the story.

By the time the DVD was released in 2002, effects technology had moved on to the point where the original models could be replaced with new computer-generated images (CGI). The DVD offers the viewer a choice of watching with the original effects or with CG replacements.

On the far left you can see the new CG version of the Ark created for the DVD release. Also shown here (left) is the original model being constructed in the BBC Visual Effects Workshop in 1974.

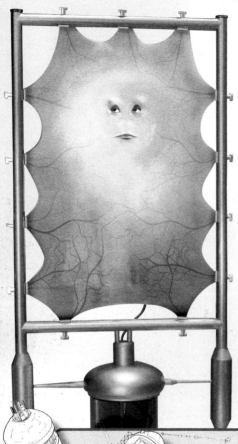

PLATFORM ONE

When the Earth was finally destroyed as the sun expanded, five billion years in the future, Platform One afforded the best view of the event.

The gravity satellites that had protected the deserted Earth from the fire of the sun for millennia were switched off when funding ran out, and various life forms gathered to watch 'Earthdeath' (followed by drinks in the platform's Manchester Suite).

Platform One was governed by the Steward, an ever-polite and diplomatic blue-skinned Crespallion, determined to ensure that the Earthdeath event went to plan and that his important guests were well catered for and at ease. He was assisted by a staff of uniformed, diminutive blue-skinned humanoids.

But when the Ninth Doctor and his new friend Rose Tyler arrived, a saboteur was already at work. Lady Cassandra – claiming to be the last pure-blood Earth human – used spindly metal robot spiders to attack the Platform's systems so it would be destroyed when the sun expanded.

Cassandra herself was by this time – after years of cosmetic and enhancement surgery, and genetic (and gender) manipulation – reduced to a thin piece of skin stretched across a metal frame. Cassandra's brain resided in a nutrient tank at the base of the frame.

The Doctor was able to save the Platform and thwart Cassandra's plans. But the Earth was destroyed on schedule, burned up as the sun swelled to engulf it…

PLATFORM ART

An immense amount of design work went into the realisation of Platform One. Before the computer-generated model of the spacestation and its shuttle craft could be started, the whole platform was rigorously designed. Everything was defined – down to where the shuttles would dock, and how the structure of the station would appear glimpsed through windows in the Manchester Suite.

The drawings and painting here show some of that world and the painstaking amount of detail put into Platform One by both the **Doctor Who** Art Department and effects house The Mill.

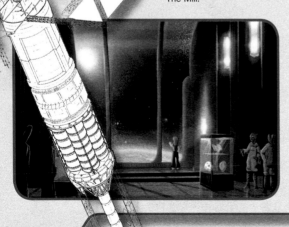

Left: A schematic of Platform One, and a painting of the interior.
Above: Another view along the length of Platform One.

Story
The End of the World
Written by
Russell T Davies
Featuring
the Ninth Doctor
and Rose
First broadcast
2 April 2005
1 episode

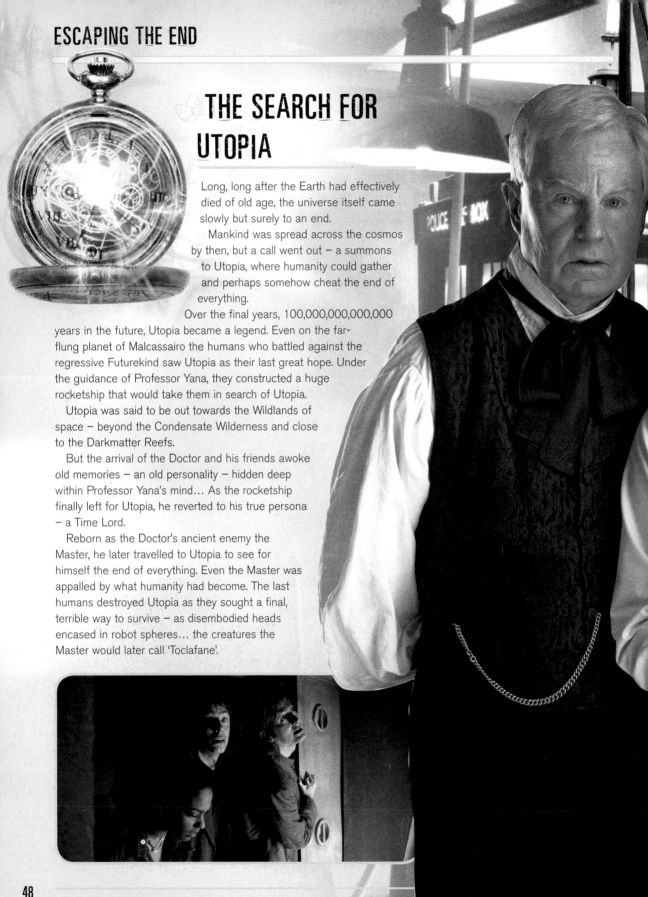

THE SEARCH FOR UTOPIA

Long, long after the Earth had effectively died of old age, the universe itself came slowly but surely to an end.

Mankind was spread across the cosmos by then, but a call went out – a summons to Utopia, where humanity could gather and perhaps somehow cheat the end of everything.

Over the final years, 100,000,000,000,000 years in the future, Utopia became a legend. Even on the far-flung planet of Malcassairo the humans who battled against the regressive Futurekind saw Utopia as their last great hope. Under the guidance of Professor Yana, they constructed a huge rocketship that would take them in search of Utopia.

Utopia was said to be out towards the Wildlands of space – beyond the Condensate Wilderness and close to the Darkmatter Reefs.

But the arrival of the Doctor and his friends awoke old memories – an old personality – hidden deep within Professor Yana's mind… As the rocketship finally left for Utopia, he reverted to his true persona – a Time Lord.

Reborn as the Doctor's ancient enemy the Master, he later travelled to Utopia to see for himself the end of everything. Even the Master was appalled by what humanity had become. The last humans destroyed Utopia as they sought a final, terrible way to survive – as disembodied heads encased in robot spheres… the creatures the Master would later call 'Toclafane'.

BUILDING UTOPIA

Like the ancient ruins of the Malmooth city which the Doctor, Martha and Jack find on Malcassairo, the huge Utopia rocketship in its enormous silo was a computer-generated image created by The Mill.

The rocketship's take-off was also achieved using computer animation. But, of course, by then the Doctor has other things on his mind…

The designs on this page show the level of detail put into the design of the images – even for the walkway, which is only seen briefly in the finished episode.

Story
Utopia
Written by
Russell T Davies
Featuring
the Tenth Doctor, Martha
and Captain Jack
First broadcast
16 June 2007
1 episode

ALIEN ENCOUNTERS

Although it was not until the twentieth century that Earth started its own space exploration and began to draw attention to itself in the universe, the planet was visited by space travellers many times throughout its history. In fact, the very existence of life on Earth was the result of a spaceship crash…

THE START OF LIFE

Escaping from their own world, the last of the warlike Jagaroth race made a forced landing on primordial Earth, approximately 400 million years ago.

The pilot of the ship – Scaroth – attempted to take off again, despite the damage, and the ship exploded. Scaroth was splintered into twelve aspects of himself, scattered through Earth's history and living independent but connected lives.

Each of these aspects of Scaroth worked to advance mankind's technological evolution to a point where the Scaroth furthest in the future – Count Scarlioni, based in twentieth-century Paris – would be able to build a time machine. He could then travel back and stop himself attempting take-off.

Although Scaroth made it back to the moment of take-off, the Doctor and Romana, with their friend Duggan, managed to stop him preventing the launch and changing history. The ship exploded – and the energy released in the blast triggered the initial evolution of life on Earth.

Story
City of Death
Written by
David Agnew
Featuring
the Fourth Doctor
and Romana
First broadcast
29 September–20
October 1979
4 episodes

MAKING PREHISTORY

The Jagaroth ship and primeval landscape were created by Ian Scoones, seen here adding final details to the model (right). On page 51 you can see the final effect – complete with model TARDIS.

INVADERS FROM MARS

Thousands of years ago, visitors from Earth's nearest neighbour came to investigate the planet. Their technology was far in advance of that of the prehistoric inhabitants of Earth. But the Martian ship crashed at the foot of a glacier.

The Martian captain, Varga, and his small crew were frozen within the glacier. Mars died – its inhabitants abandoning it when life there became untenable.

By the year 3,000, the Earth was in the grip of a new ice age. Britannicus Base was at the forefront of the battle to turn back the glaciers.

The base was a magnificent Georgian mansion, preserved within a protective bubble. Commanded by Leader Clent, the scientists at Britannicus struggled to hold back the ice using an ioniser to intensify the heat of the sun on the landscape.

But as well as driving back the ice, the ioniser freed the Martian ship. The armoured 'Ice Warriors' trapped inside were revived, and saw the ioniser as a weapon and the humans at Britannicus Base as their enemies.

Story
The Ice Warriors
Written by
Brian Hayles
Featuring
the Second Doctor,
Jamie and Victoria
First broadcast
11 November–16
December 1967
6 episodes

VOLCANO DAY

One of the stranger visits to Earth was the arrival of a group of Pyroviles in Italy in the year 79 AD. Escaping from the loss of Pyrovillia, the creatures were a race made of rock and fire, and all their technology derived from these same elements.

Making their base deep inside the volcano Vesuvius, the Pyroviles planned to harness the heat of the Earth itself and weld themselves to humans – creating a new species that would establish a mighty empire. The Earth would become their home, the oceans and seas boiled away in the tremendous heat.

Faced with the terrible knowledge that saving the world meant sacrificing Pompeii, the Doctor was only able to defeat the Pyroviles with the help of his friend Donna Noble. They inverted the Pyroviles' systems, turning the power of the volcano back against them. As history records, Vesuvius erupted with the force of 24 nuclear bombs. It was only thanks to the incredible resilience of the Pyrovile escape pod where they took refuge that the Doctor and Donna escaped the destruction.

Story
The Fires of Pompeii
Written by
James Moran
Featuring
the Tenth Doctor
and Donna
First broadcast
12 April 2008
1 episode

RECREATING POMPEII

Faced with the task of recreating ancient Pompeii, the **Doctor Who** team actually went to Italy – though not to Pompeii itself. Instead, they spent two days in 2007 shooting on the lavish studio sets used for the HBO TV series **Rome**. Parts of the studio were damaged by fire before the **Doctor Who** team arrived, but luckily none of the areas used for Pompeii were affected.

The footage shot in Rome was combined with location and studio work from much closer to the programme's Cardiff home, but the end result was a totally believable ancient Roman environment.

Combined with The Mill's stunning digital effects for the Pyrovile creatures and the eruption of Vesuvius, Pompeii became a tour-de-force of spectacular design.

LIGHTING THE FIRES

The effect of people turning to stone was achieved with make-up and special prosthetics provided by Millennium FX. But, like the explosion of Vesuvius itself, the Pyrovile fire creatures were created by The Mill as computer-generated images.

The fire element made the creatures more difficult to design and realise than more straightforward rock monsters would have been. But when combined with live action footage shot on location and on the lavish sets of Pompeii, the effect was startling and frighteningly realistic. The Pyroviles are a worthy addition to the ranks of CG enemies the Doctor has faced.

CAPTAIN JACK HARKNESS

One of many visitors to Earth from another planet or time, Captain Jack Harkness (as he calls himself) never intended to invade or take over the planet. When he first arrived during the Second World War, he was actually planning to sell space junk to a Time Agent, pretending it was a Chula Warship.

The 'junk' that Jack sent crashing to Earth was actually a Chula ambulance filled with nanogenes – subatomic robots that checked the ship's occupants for damage which they then repaired.

The nanogenes had never before come into contact with a human, so didn't understand the physiognomy. Escaping from the crashed ship, the nanogenes sought a human 'template' from

Story
The Empty Child &
The Doctor Dances
Written by
Steven Moffat
Featuring
the Ninth Doctor, Rose
and Captain Jack
First broadcast
21–28 May 2005
2 episodes

which to 'repair' all others they came into contact with. This was a small boy killed in an earlier air raid, and wearing his gas mask. As a result, the nanogenes began to remodel the entire human race on a terrified child searching for its mother, and equipped to fight as a Chula warrior.

Jack's own spacecraft was actually a Chula warship, which he had stolen. It had a tractor beam – like a searchlight – which he used to catch Rose when she fell from a barrage balloon during an air raid. The ship could become invisible using an active camouflage system. To make sure he could find it again, Jack tethered the invisible ship to the Clock Tower of the Palace of Westminster (which houses Big Ben). The emergency teleport was security-keyed to Jack's molecular structure, and using the ship's om-com system he could transmit his voice to anything with a speaker grille.

THE CHULA AMBULANCE

The Chula ship was a large mauve cylinder – mauve being the universally recognised colour for danger (humans are an exception in using red). The ship was actually the equivalent of an ambulance, deployed to the battlefield to repair Chula Warriors injured in combat. It fell on Limehouse Green Station and was immediately cordoned off and placed under guard.

Jack claimed the ship was a fully equipped Chula Warship – the last one in existence. He arranged for it to land in a spot where it would soon be destroyed by a German bomb.

Jack's plan was to sell the ship to the Time Agency, and when he first met her he thought Rose was a Time Agent. Jack deliberately steered the ambulance cylinder close to the TARDIS so the 'Time Agents' would see it and follow it down.

THE LONG HAUL

Alien timescales are often very different to the human concept of time. This has meant that some aliens have spent a long time on Earth before their nefarious plans have been fully realised. Sometimes this is through choice, sometimes by chance.

DEATH WISH

Story Mawdryn Undead ⚙ Written by Peter Grimwade
⚙ Featuring the Fifth Doctor, Nyssa, Tegan, Turlough and Brigadier
Lethbridge-Stewart (rtd) ⚙ First broadcast 1–9 February 1983 ⚙ 4 episodes

The mutant humanoids led by Mawdryn spent 3,000 years in a warp ellipse orbit, guided to a nearby planet once every 70 years. Who knows how many times their elliptical orbit drew them close to Earth? It was here that the Fifth Doctor encountered them – travelling between Earth and the ship via a transmat.

In Mawdryn's case, he and his colleagues had been exiled by the Elders of their planet after stealing Time Lord technology and trying to extend their lives. Only with the help of the Doctor and his friends – including the Doctor's old colleague Brigadier Lethbridge-Stewart – could Mawdryn and the others finally die, their ship exploding when it had no further use.

PRISON SHIP

Story The Stones of Blood ⚙ Written by David Fisher
⚙ Featuring the Fourth Doctor, Romana and K-9
⚙ First broadcast 28 October–18 November 1978 ⚙ 4 episodes

When Cessair of Diplos was captured after stealing the Great Seal of Diplos, she was incarcerated with the stone Ogri creatures she had taken from the planet Ogros. They were locked in cells on a prison ship and sent to stand trial. Travelling on the same ship were the Megara justice machines that would supervise that trial.

But the ship never arrived. Cessair escaped and

fled to Earth with the Ogri. The ship was left stranded in hyperspace above the stone circle where Cessair placed the Ogri – until the Doctor discovered its existence and the Megara eventually found Cessair guilty as charged.

THE ZYGON GAMBIT

Story Terror of the Zygons ☻ Written by Robert Banks Stewart
☻ Featuring the Fourth Doctor, Sarah, Harry and UNIT
☻ First broadcast 30 August–20 September 1975 ☻ 4 episodes

A group of Zygons also spent time hidden on Earth. Their ship crashed into Loch Ness centuries ago, and they hid under the water together with the huge reptilian Skarasen that provided them with sustenance.

Learning that their own planet had been destroyed in a stellar explosion, Broton – warlord of the Zygons – decided to use the powerful cyborg Skarasen to conquer Earth. The Zygons could then transform the planet into a world where the refugee Zygons from their own planet could settle. Unable to persuade Broton to share the Earth with its human population, the Doctor destroyed the Zygon ship.

Only the Skarasen survived – returning to its home in Loch Ness to live in peace…

GABRIEL CHASE

Story Ghostlight ☻ Written by Marc Platt
☻ Featuring the Seventh Doctor and Ace
☻ First broadcast 4–18 October 1989 ☻ 3 episodes

The creature known as Light endured another inadvertent stay on Earth. Arriving in prehistoric times to catalogue all life, Light slept in his ship while the survey took place. Light's ship was eventually built into the cellar of a house called Gabriel Chase, and the life form that constituted the survey woke, imprisoned its Control, and evolved into a human calling himself Josiah Samuel Smith.

When Light also woke, he was unable to cope with the concept of evolution – and the fact that as life evolved and changed his survey could never be completed.

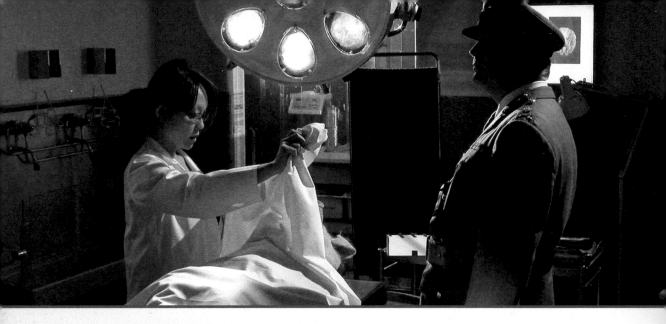

⊛ FLYING SPACE PIG

When a spaceship crash-landed in the Thames after colliding with the Clock Tower that houses Big Ben at the Palace of Westminster, it seemed to signal the arrival of aliens on Earth. But as the Doctor noted, the crash-landing was just too perfect – from the angle of descent to the colour of the trailing smoke.

Investigating further, he discovered that the crash had been staged by the Slitheen. They wanted to draw attention away from their initial arrival some time earlier in the North Sea, and to lure the world's experts on extraterrestrial incursion to London…

As part of their deception, the Slitheen created a fake alien life form out of an ordinary farmyard pig. They dressed it in a spacesuit and left it to be found in the crashed ship. The pig was taken to Albion Hospital, where it was examined by Toshiko Sato from Torchwood Three. The pig had been augmented with Slitheen technology – its brain had been 'wired up' and components had been added to convince investigators that it was a real alien. The Doctor likened the pig to a Victorian fairground 'mermaid', cobbled together as a hoax.

Despite the Doctor's attempts to befriend it, the terrified pig was shot by one of the soldiers guarding the hospital.

The Doctor and Rose, with help from Mickey and from future Prime Minister Harriet Jones, were able to stop the Slitheen from destroying the world with nuclear weapons.

Story
Aliens of London &
World War Three
Written by
Russell T Davies
Featuring
the Ninth Doctor, Rose
and Mickey
First broadcast
16–23 April 2005
2 episodes

THE CHRISTMAS STAR

The star that appeared over London at Christmas was in fact a Racnoss Webstar spaceship. Piloted by the last of the Racnoss – their Empress – it fired on the city of London before being shot down by a tank on the orders of Mr Saxon.

The Empress of the Racnoss was searching for another Webstar, the *Secret Heart*, which was lost billions of years ago back in the Dark Times. In fact, the planet Earth formed round it. The Racnoss were all but destroyed by the Fledgling Empires, only their Empress and the *Secret Heart* surviving.

Racnoss young were born starving, and the Racnoss from the *Secret Heart* would have devoured the Earth and its people if the Doctor and his friend Donna had not managed to defeat the Empress and drown her children with water from the River Thames.

Story
The Runaway Bride
Written by
Russell T Davies
Featuring
**the Tenth Doctor
and Donna**
First broadcast
**25 December 2006
1 episode**

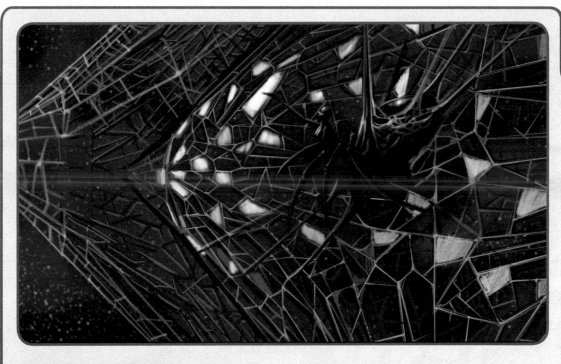

STAR QUALITY

Like many other spaceships in **Doctor Who**, the Racnoss Webstar was created as a computer-generated image, created by effects company The Mill.

The Racnoss Empress herself, however, was a full-size prop into which actress Sarah Parish was fitted. It was designed and built by Millennium FX, and was so large it was only fully assembled for the first time when it was taken on location for *The Runaway Bride*.

MOON LANDING

The mercenary law-enforcement race the Judoon used an H_2O scoop to transport a whole hospital, the Royal Hope, from London to the moon in order to arrest a criminal Plasmavore. Disguised as one of the hospital's patients – an old lady called Florence Finnegan – the Plasmavore was

SPECIES IDENTIFIER

TORCH HOUSING

GRIP TWISTS
TO ACTIVATE

10
cm

BASE SHEATH
SLIDES UP TO
REVEAL MARKER

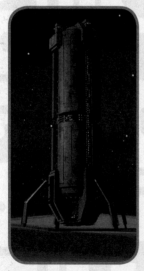

TRANSLATING DESIGNS

The shape of the Judoon ships shows just how integrated the design is of every element of **Doctor Who**. While different designers, and even different companies, work on various aspects of the series, the whole 'look' of **Doctor Who** as a whole and of each individual story is agreed by everyone involved. A 'tone meeting' is held for each story where the overall look and approach is decided.

The fact that the Judoon spaceship – a computer-generated image created by The Mill – and the Judoon hand-held scanner – a physical 'lifesize' prop – are similar in appearance is a reflection of the degree to which this overall design approach works. Both spaceship and scanner are obviously derived from the same technology designed by a single alien race – the Judoon.

Episode
Smith and Jones
Written by
Russell T Davies
Featuring
the Tenth Doctor
and Martha
First broadcast
31 March 2007
1 episode

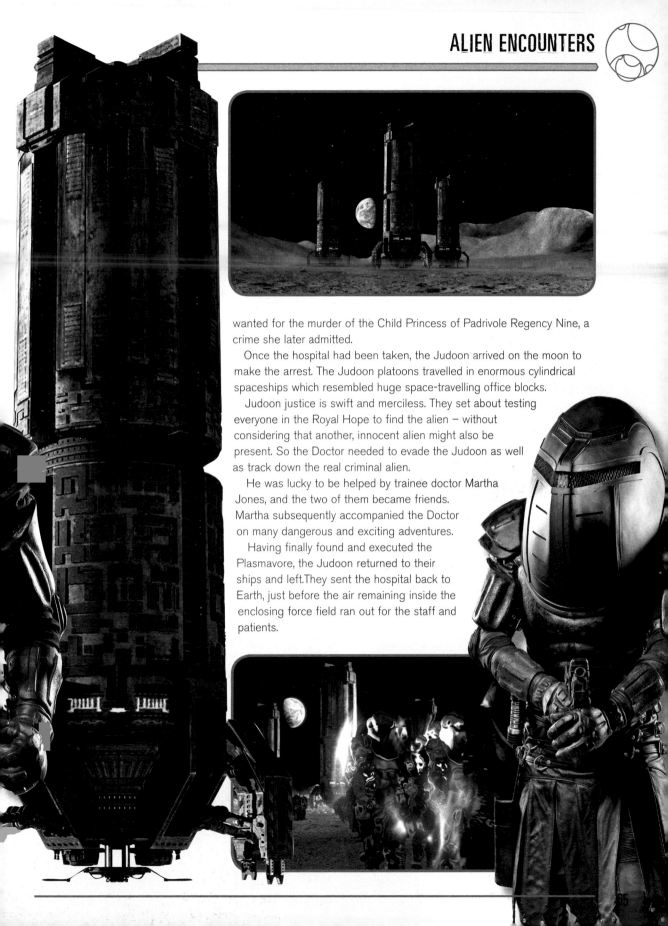

wanted for the murder of the Child Princess of Padrivole Regency Nine, a crime she later admitted.

Once the hospital had been taken, the Judoon arrived on the moon to make the arrest. The Judoon platoons travelled in enormous cylindrical spaceships which resembled huge space-travelling office blocks.

Judoon justice is swift and merciless. They set about testing everyone in the Royal Hope to find the alien – without considering that another, innocent alien might also be present. So the Doctor needed to evade the Judoon as well as track down the real criminal alien.

He was lucky to be helped by trainee doctor Martha Jones, and the two of them became friends. Martha subsequently accompanied the Doctor on many dangerous and exciting adventures.

Having finally found and executed the Plasmavore, the Judoon returned to their ships and left. They sent the hospital back to Earth, just before the air remaining inside the enclosing force field ran out for the staff and patients.

SYCORAX ATTACK

The so-called Christmas invasion took the Earth by surprise. The first the world knew of the arrival of the Sycorax was when they captured and destroyed the unmanned *Guinevere One* probe. In fact, there was no invasion – rather an attempt by the Sycorax to blackmail the world leaders into surrender by taking hypnotic 'blood control' of everyone with an A+ blood type.

The Sycorax are a race of scavengers, from the asteroid they call Fire Trap, though that was destroyed long ago. Legend has it that the Sycorax will – with humanity – survive until the end of the universe.

Sycorax spaceships are hewn from rock and decorated with trophies of their victories and conquests.

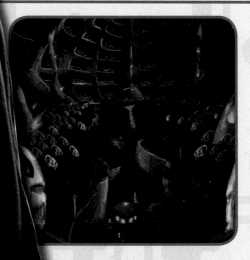

ROCK PAINTING

The pictures here show the level of detail and thought put into every aspect of the Sycorax ship. Much of the detail in the finished set – like the remains of a prisoner hanging in a cage – was barely noticeable on screen, there was so much of it.

Story
The Christmas Invasion
Written by
Russell T Davies
Featuring
the Tenth Doctor
and Rose
First broadcast
25 December 2005
1 episode

THE FAMILY OF BLOOD

An incursion rather than an invasion, the Family of Blood came to Earth in 1913, hunting for the Doctor. A short-lived species, they wanted to absorb the Doctor's Time Lord essence so that they could live for ever.

The Doctor was in hiding on Earth at a public school in Herefordshire in England, where he was working as a history teacher, John Smith. This was not just a disguise – the Doctor had used a 'chameleon arch' to alter his physical form and his own memories so that he actually *was* John Smith. His plan was to stay in hiding until the Family of Blood died, rather than have to deal with them.

But the Family found the Doctor and brought local scarecrows to life as eerie troops in their battle against the Doctor and his colleagues and pupils at Farringham School.

Little is known about the Family's spaceship, partly because they rendered it invisible when they landed to escape detection. It seemed to be an organic craft, within which the Family changed their own appearances by taking over the bodies of local villagers. The ship was destroyed when the Doctor defeated the Family.

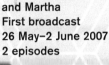

Story
Human Nature &
The Family of Blood
Written by
Paul Cornell
Featuring
the Tenth Doctor
and Martha
First broadcast
26 May–2 June 2007
2 episodes

CAPRICORN CRUISES

In its heyday, Max Capricorn Cruiseliners offered the pinnacle of luxury. Providing comfort and service in the styles of the less advanced planets they visited, the liners' cruises were expensive and exclusive. Passengers could visit planets by teleport, seeing the sights and shopping for souvenirs, before continuing to the next port of call.

Despite the popularity of its cruises, the business got into financial difficulties, and Max Capricorn was voted off the board of his own company.

Determined to get revenge and to retire in style, Max Capricorn planned to crash one of his own liners – the *Titanic*, en route from the planet Sto – into the Earth. The new company board would be liable, and Max Capricorn could take money

Story
Voyage of the Damned
Written by
Russell T Davies
Featuring
**the Tenth Doctor
and Astrid**
First broadcast
**25 December 2007
1 episode**

from secret accounts to retire to the beaches of Penhaxico Two. One reason for this choice of retirement home was that Capricorn had been forced to become a cyborg – part robot – to stay alive. While cyborgs were despised in his own society, they were welcomed elsewhere…

To ensure that his plan worked, Capricorn blackmailed the captain of the *Titanic* to deactivate its shields just before a meteoroid strike. He also reprogrammed the Heavenly Host robots that acted as servants and information centres on the *Titanic* so that they would kill any surviving passengers and crew to ensure the ship could not be saved.

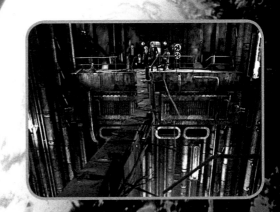

But Capricorn had not expected the Doctor. Arriving on the *Titanic* just before the meteoroid strike, the Doctor managed to stop the ship from crashing. With help from the few survivors, the Doctor found Max Capricorn himself hiding onboard in an omnistate impact chamber. Capricorn was killed when waitress Astrid Peth gave her own life to save the *Titanic* and the people on the Earth below. The Doctor was unable to save Astrid, though he did manage to convert her to stardust so she could travel through the incredible sights of the universe for ever…

The *Titanic* itself was modelled on a famous Earth ocean cruiser of the same name. But a lack of detailed research meant that the crew were unaware that the original *Titanic* sank on its first voyage in 1912 after striking an iceberg.

RAISING THE TITANIC

The beautiful *Titanic* space cruiser was a computer-generated image created by The Mill. The designs on these pages show some of the initial paintings from which The Mill then designed the *Titanic*, as well as sketches and paintings of the lavish interior of the ship. *Voyage of the Damned* was made on location and in the studio, so the cast and crew never actually put to sea (or went into space).

FAT CHANCE

Not long after Max Capricorn's *Titanic* almost crashed into Buckingham Palace, the people of London witnessed the arrival of another spaceship. This time, the aliens had come not to conquer or populate Earth, but to take something away – their children.

Adipose Industries, headed by the sinister Miss Foster, offered a revolutionary way of losing weight. A capsule containing a synthesised mobilising lipase bound to a large protein molecule broke down the fat and flushed it away in the bloodstream – or so Miss Foster claimed.

As the Doctor and Donna found out when investigating the company, the capsules did nothing of the sort. They actually gathered and bound the fat together to make a small body – an Adipose.

Miss Foster was in fact Matron Cofelia of the Five-Straighten Classabindi Nursery Fleet (intergalactic class). She had been employed by the Adiposian First Family to foster a new generation of Adipose children, after their breeding planet was lost. Over a million people had been taking the capsules, Adipose children being created out of their excess fat. But Miss Foster didn't intend to let it end there. The Adipose could also convert whole human bodies – bone, organs, hair – into Adipose material…

The Doctor and Donna were able to stop the conversion before it went too far, and Adiposian ships arrived to take away the Adipose children.

Story
Partners in Crime
Written by
Russell T Davies
Featuring
the Tenth Doctor
and Donna
First broadcast
5 April 2008
1 episode

WEIGHTY DESIGN

The Adipose spaceship was designed and created as a computer-generated effect by The Mill. They were also responsible for the small Adipose child creatures created out of people's excess body fat.

SPACECRAFT OF THE UNIVERSE

The influence of the human race on the history of the universe as a whole is undeniable. But as well as the spaceships of Earth's developing space programmes, the alien craft that have visited Earth over the years and the warships of would-be invaders, there are of course hundreds and thousands of other starships and spacestations in the cosmos.

These range from the burrowing camouflage ships of the Movellans to the organic egg-ships of the Tythonians, and from the functional craft of the Jocondans to the size-changing ships of the ancient Dæmons. There is not the time or the space in a volume like this to itemise and describe them all.

But in this section we describe some of the more notable spacecraft the Doctor has encountered on his travels.

KROTONS' DYNOTROPE

> Story The Krotons ○ Written by Robert Holmes
> ○ Featuring the Second Doctor, Jamie and Zoe
> ○ First broadcast 28 December 1968–18 January 1969 ○ 4 episodes

The Krotons' spaceship was stranded for centuries on the planet of the Gonds, while a whole society grew up around it, ignorant of its true nature.

By the time the Doctor and his friends arrived, the crashed Krotons' Dynotrope had been set in perpetual stability to preserve power. The ship's systems were used to educate the primitive humanoid Gonds to the level the ship needed to reanimate the surviving Krotons, which were fed their mental energy.

The energy derived from the Doctor and Zoe when they took the Krotons' tests was enough to revive the crystalline creatures, which had been stored as an inert crystalline slurry. The Doctor helped the Gonds to destroy the Kroton ship with acid before the Krotons could fully power up and destroy the Gonds.

STARFALL SEVEN

> Story The Face of Evil ○ Written by Chris Boucher
> ○ Featuring the Fourth Doctor and Leela
> ○ First broadcast 1–22 January 1977 ○ 4 episodes

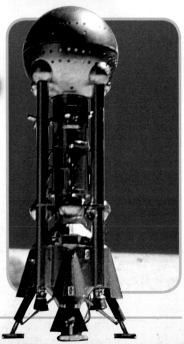

As space travel increased, so too did the number of expeditions which ran into trouble, or which simply vanished.

One of the most curious of these incidents was the disappearance of the Mordee Expedition. Experimenting with the ship's computer, the crew turned it into a super-being called Xoanon.

But, as a result of the Doctor programming it using a Sidelian memory transfer, Xoanon developed a split personality. The Doctor forgot to wipe his own personality from the computer, which played out its schizophrenia using the ship's technicians and survey teams and setting them against each other…

It took another intervention from the Fourth Doctor to resolve the situation and 'cure' Xoanon.

ARMAGEDDON

Story The Armageddon Factor ○ Written by Bob Baker
and Dave Martin ○ Featuring the Fourth Doctor,
Romana and K-9 ○ First broadcast 20 January–24 February 1979 ○ 6 episodes

The devastation that can be wreaked on a planet by space war is nowhere
more apparent than in the conflict between the twin planets Atrios and
Zeos. Atrios was all but destroyed by nuclear bombardment, its population
forced to live in shelters far below the planet's surface. The Zeons were
wiped out.

Ultimately, the war was a disaster for both sides – a tragedy
compounded by the fact it was manipulated by the creature known as the
Shadow in his quest to find the final segment of the Key to Time before
the Doctor could recover it. Only when the Key had been recovered was
the Doctor able to bring the war to an end…

ETERNAL SPACE TRAVEL

Story Enlightenment ○ Written by Barbara Clegg
○ Featuring the Fifth Doctor, Tegan and Turlough
○ First broadcast 1–9 March 1983 ○ 4 episodes

By contrast, the craft the Eternals used in their celebrated race for
Enlightenment were beautiful space-sailing ships from different periods of
Earth's history rather than functional weapons of war.

But despite the beauty and elegance of their ships, the Eternals
themselves were dangerous creatures who saw the ephemeral humans
with which they crewed their craft as mere playthings, to be used and
discarded on a whim.

The Eternals were creatures living outside time in the never-ending realm
of eternity itself. Nothing mattered to them save the excitement of the race
and the promise of the prize at its end. Anything to alleviate the crushing
boredom of eternity.

GAZTAK ATTACK

Story Meglos ◌ Written by John Flanagan and Andrew McCulloch
◌ Featuring the Fourth Doctor, Romana and K-9
◌ First broadcast 27 September–18 October 1980 ◌ 4 episodes

At the opposite end of the scale of elegance from the sailing ships of the Eternals were the bland and functional craft favoured by those marauding bands of space mercenaries called Gaztaks.

Few Gaztaks were more greedy – or incompetent – than General Grugger's crew. Grugger and his lieutenant, Brotadac, met their final end on the dead planet of Zolfa-Thura. They had been hired to help the last Zolfa-Thuran, Meglos – a Xerophyte.

Meglos even went so far as to impersonate the Doctor to reclaim the Dodecahedron that would power the mysterious Screens of Zolfa-Thura and turn them into a powerful weapon. But the Doctor turned the weapon back on Zolfa-Thura and the planet was destroyed.

WAR FLEET

Story The Dominators ◌ Written by Norman Ashby
◌ Featuring the Second Doctor, Jamie and Zoe
◌ First broadcast 10 August–7 September 1968 ◌ 5 episodes

Time and again the Doctor has been caught up in the military ambitions of other races. The cruel Dominators and their brutal Quark robots destroyed planets to create supplies of fuel for their war fleet.

The Doctor was able to save the peaceful planet Dulkis from Dominators Rago and Toba, but who knows how many other planets have fallen to the Dominators, their peoples enslaved.

MONARCH OF THE SKIES

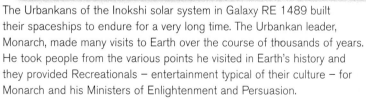

Story Four to Doomsday ◌ Written by Terence Dudley
◌ Featuring the Fifth Doctor, Adric, Nyssa and Tegan
◌ First broadcast 18–26 January 1982 ◌ 4 episodes

The Urbankans of the Inokshi solar system in Galaxy RE 1489 built their spaceships to endure for a very long time. The Urbankan leader, Monarch, made many visits to Earth over the course of thousands of years. He took people from the various points he visited in Earth's history and they provided Recreationals – entertainment typical of their culture – for Monarch and his Ministers of Enlightenment and Persuasion.

His human specimens had long since died and were now preserved as memories on microchips inside humanoid computers and overseen by Monarch using spherical robotic monopticons. Monarch planned to destroy the Earth on his next visit, looting its minerals to speed up his ship so it could travel faster than light and travel back in time. Monarch believed he was the original creator of the universe, and he wanted to meet himself. But the Doctor was able to prevent him from reaching Earth.

THE EDGE OF SPACE

> Story Planet of Evil ◌ Written by Louis Marks
> ◌ Featuring the Fourth Doctor and Sarah
> ◌ First broadcast 27 September–18 October 1975 ◌ 4 episodes

The Morestrans also travelled to the very limits of the unknown. Their scientific expedition to Zeta Minor almost ended in the destruction of the universe itself. Professor Sorenson believed he had discovered a material that would provide energy to fuel the dying Morestran sun. Sorenson became infected with anti-matter, becoming a murderous, primeval monster.

Arriving at the same time as the Morestran probe sent to rescue Sorenson, the Doctor discovered that Zeta Minor was a planet on the very edge of creation – a gateway to the universe of anti-matter. With the probe struggling to escape the planet, the Doctor had to persuade the Morestrans that taking anti-matter from the planet would cause radiation annihilation.

THE MIGHTY SKONNON EMPIRE

> Story The Horns of Nimon ◌ Written by Anthony Read
> ◌ Featuring the Fourth Doctor, Romana and K-9
> ◌ First broadcast 22 December 1979–12 January 1980 ◌ 4 episodes

The rise and fall and attempted rise again of the Skonnon Empire is well documented. Skonnos was once the heart of an empire that extended over a hundred star systems, but that empire was lost in a civil war that only the army survived.

The last gasp of the Skonnon Empire came under the leadership of scientist Soldeed. He allied himself with the Nimon, which promised him the means of building a fleet that would restore Skonnon superiority. But the Nimon were a scavenger race that offered help to planets while they opened a black hole gateway from their previous conquest. Hundreds of Nimon would then stream through and ravage their former allies.

JOURNEY TO TERRADON

> Story Full Circle ◌ Written by Andrew Smith
> ◌ Featuring the Fourth Doctor, Romana, Adric and K-9
> ◌ First broadcast 25 October–15 November 1980 ◌ 4 episodes

The more peaceful Terradonians travelled to the world of Alzarius in the Exo-Space time continuum, a smaller universe separate from our own. When the *Starliner* crashed, the crew were all killed by native Alzarians. But the way life on Alzarius rapidly evolved to suit its changing environment meant that these 'Marshmen' took on the form of the original crew they had replaced. They tried to repair the ship under the guidance of the ruling Deciders and, over the years, they came to believe they were Terradonians.

The Doctor's arrival coincided with the fabled time of Mistfall, when the evolutionary cycle began again. Grotesque creatures rose from the marshes and huge poisonous spiders hatched from riverfruit…

THE MINYAN QUEST

Story Underworld ◌ Written by Bob Baker and Dave Martin
◌ Featuring the Fourth Doctor, Leela and K-9
◌ First broadcast 7–28 January 1978 ◌ 4 episodes

Surviving against all odds were the people of Minyos – a planet destroyed 100,000 years ago.

The Minyans saved race banks so they could preserve their species. Captain Jackson and his crew were sent in the *R1C* to find the ship carrying the race banks – the *P7E*. They had the ability to regenerate, but after such a long quest were tired and on the point of giving up when they finally found the planet that had formed round the *P7E* at the edge of the universe. The *P7E*'s computer – the Oracle – now ruled the underworld regime populated by the descendents of the original crew, and obsessively guarded the Minyan race banks.

ZANAK – THE PIRATE PLANET

Story The Pirate Planet ◌ Written by Douglas Adams
◌ Featuring the Fourth Doctor, Romana and K-9
◌ First broadcast 30 September–21 October 1978 ◌ 4 episodes

Zanak was a happy prosperous planet until the reign of Queen Xanxia, who lived for hundreds of years. Towards the end of her reign, the Captain arrived – falling from the sky in a mighty ship called the *Ventilianus*.

The planet was hollowed out and fitted with huge transmat engines by the mysterious Captain. Zanak could then space-jump to land around another smaller planet. This planet was in turn mined for its wealth – the population obviously being killed in the initial 'attack'.

When the Doctor and Romana discovered the truth, they were horrified. With the Captain and Xanxia both finally dead, and Zanak's engine room destroyed, the planet settled down to a more conventional existence.

CYBER SHIPS

Centuries ago, on Earth's twin planet Mondas, a race of men sought immortality. They replaced their failing limbs and organs with plastic and steel. They exchanged their brains for computers and eliminated all feeling and emotion from their systems. The resulting Cybermen were immensely strong, and determined to survive, no matter what the cost to other life forms.

Over the centuries, as the Cybermen moved from Mondas to a new planet – Telos – and even when they developed on a parallel version of Earth in another universe, Cyber technology changed and developed, and the Cybermen made use of whatever materials they could find and adapt. But throughout, their spacecraft remained functional and efficient, with no thought or consideration for comfort.

ATTEMPTED INVASION

> Story The Invasion ☺ Written by Derrick Sherwin (from a story by Kit Pedler)
> ☺ Featuring the Second Doctor, Jamie, Zoe and UNIT
> ☺ 2 November–21 December 1968 ☺ 8 episodes

The first time Cybermen came into direct contact with humans was during their attempted invasion of Earth in the 1970s. Working through Tobias Vaughn of International Electromatics, the Cybermen paralysed humanity with a hypnotic signal. But the Doctor disabled the transmitter and an army of Cybermen hidden in the London sewers was destroyed. The Cyber fleet was shot down by the British military, while UNIT helped Russian forces destroy the Cyber flagship.

CYBER SAUCERS

> Story The Moonbase ☺ Written by Kit Pedler
> ☺ Featuring the Second Doctor, Polly, Ben and Jamie
> ☺ First broadcast 11 February–4 March 1967 ☺ 4 episodes

In their two subsequent invasion attempts, the Cybermen deployed saucer-shaped Cyberships.

In 1986, their planet Mondas – Earth's 'twin' – returned to the solar system and drained power from Earth. The Cybermen landed in force across the world, but it was at the South Pole that they were defeated by the Doctor and his friends at International Space Command's Snowcap Base. (For more information, see p.6.)

The Cybermen waited almost a century – until 2070 – before they next attempted to invade Earth. This time, they relied on stealth, landing their ships on the moon and infiltrating the Lunar Weather Control Station. They planned to use the Gravitron that controlled Earth's weather to disrupt life prior to their invasion. But the Doctor was able to turn the device against the Cybermen, who were shot off into deep space.

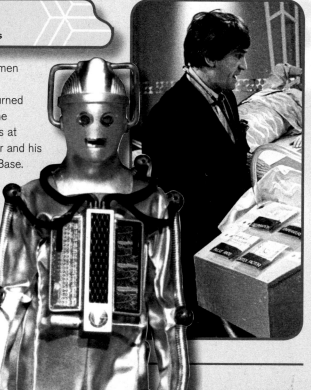

THE NEMESIS INCURSION

Story Silver Nemesis ☉ Written by Kevin Clarke
☉ Featuring the Seventh Doctor and Ace
☉ First broadcast 23 November–7 December 1988 ☉ 3 episodes

In the late 1980s, a small raiding force arrived just outside Windsor in search of the Nemesis – a statue fashioned from a living metal called Validium. The Doctor had launched the statue into space in 1638, and it then circled the Earth until its return on 23 November 1988.

While their incursion force arrived on Earth, a cloaked Cyber fleet remained close by. When the Nemesis was launched into the heart of the fleet and achieved critical mass, the Cyber fleet was destroyed.

PLANET OF GOLD

Story Revenge of the Cybermen ☉ Written by Gerry Davis
☉ Featuring the Fourth Doctor, Sarah and Harry
☉ First broadcast 19 April–10 May 1975 ☉ 4 episodes

During the terrible Cyber War, the humans defeated the Cybermen with the 'glitter gun'. This fired liquid gold which in effect suffocated the Cybermen. The huge amount of gold needed to win the war was supplied from Voga, the so-called Planet of Gold. At the end of the war, the Cybermen all but destroyed Voga. The planet's remains then drifted until caught by Jupiter's gravity, while its survivors hid in an underground survival chamber.

One of the last groups of Cybermen took over the nearby beacon, *Nerva*. Having survived the war in an ancient Cybership armed with nose-cone missile tubes, the Cybermen killed most of *Nerva*'s human crew. Ultimately, their ship was shot down by a Vogan Sky-Striker missile.

PARALLEL HISTORY

The most spectacular and deadly Cyber invasion of Earth utilised no spacecraft at all. A race of Cybermen that had developed on a parallel world to Earth in another universe broke through the cracks between universes created by a Dalek Void Ship (see p.90).

Millions of Cybermen arrived on Earth, first as vague outlines – an army of ghosts. But the Cybermen then came through fully, intent on invading our Earth as they were driven from their own dying world.

The Doctor managed to defeat both the Cybermen and the Daleks from the Void Ship. But at a terrible cost.

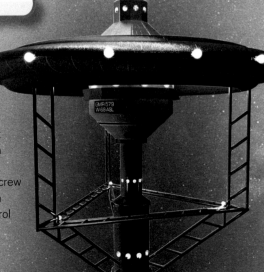

EARTHSHOCK FREIGHTER

Story Earthshock ☺ Written by Eric Saward
☺ Featuring the Fifth Doctor, Adric, Nyssa and Tegan
☺ First broadcast 8–16 March 1982 ☺ 4 episodes

With a conference due to take place on Earth to establish an alliance against the Cybermen, and knowing they could not hope to penetrate Earth's defences during the conference, the Cybermen planted a bomb long in advance in an isolated cave system. In the confusion and devastation caused by the explosion, a force of Cybermen would land, hidden in the cargo of a space freighter.

But the bomb was discovered and defused by the Doctor, assisted by a military team which destroyed the androids left to guard the caves.

The Cybermen then smashed out of the silos on the freighter where they were hidden and took control, planning to crash the ship into Earth. Stopping the Cybermen cost the life of the Doctor's friend Adric.

STATION THREE

Story The Wheel in Space ☺ Written by David Whitaker
(from a story by Kit Pedler) ☺ Featuring the Second Doctor, Jamie and Zoe
☺ First broadcast 27 April–1 June 1968 ☺ 6 episodes

Also known as 'the Wheel', Station Three (call sign LX88J) acted as a radio-visual relay for Earth, a halfway house for deep-space ships, a space research station and stellar early warning station for all types of space phenomena staffed by a multinational crew.

The Cybermen took over the *Silver Carrier*, a Phoenix Mark IV service and supply ship for Station Five operated by a Servo Robot. It had been reported overdue nine weeks previously and was 87 million miles off course when it reached Station Three. Desperate for vital Bernalium supplies, which could be found on the *Silver Carrier*, the crew of the Wheel unwittingly brought onboard Cybermen who had been hidden in egg-like membranes. With the Wheel under Cyber control and the main force of Cybermen arriving, the Doctor managed to destroy the Cybership with the Wheel's X-ray laser.

DALEK SHIPS

Survivors of a thousand-year war on the planet Skaro, the Dalek creatures exist inside armoured protective shells. Imbued with a vicious hatred of all other life forms, the Daleks are determined to conquer the universe.

The history of the Daleks is inextricably linked with the histories of two other races – humanity and the Time Lords. The Daleks have fought against both, waging terrible war on the human race throughout eternity and engaging in the Great Time War against the Time Lords – a war that neither side could ever truly win…

DALEK PRODUCTION

> Story The Power of the Daleks ☉ Written by David Whitaker
> ☉ Featuring the Second Doctor, Polly and Ben
> ☉ First broadcast 5 November–10 December 1966 ☉ 6 episodes

There is some evidence that the Daleks' temporal engineering may extend to dimensional transcendentalism – the ability to create craft that are bigger inside than outside. When a space capsule was found buried in the mercury swamps of the human colony planet Vulcan, the threat posed by the three dormant Daleks found inside was not realised. Despite the Doctor's warnings, the human scientist Lesterson reactivated the Daleks and provided them with a static electrical power source.

Inside their ship, the Daleks set up a production-line system to produce Dalek casings, into which incubated Dalek creatures were placed. The resulting Dalek army then emerged to exterminate all human life on Vulcan.

STANDARD DALEK CRAFT

> Story The Daleks' Master Plan ☉ Written by Terry Nation and Dennis Spooner
> ☉ Featuring the First Doctor, Steven and Katarina
> ☉ First broadcast 13 November 1965–29 January 1966 ☉ 12 episodes

Although there are variations, the standard design of the Dalek spacecraft is based on the classic saucer shape. There are exceptions to this, of course, as Dalek design is first and foremost functional and efficient.

By the year 4000 AD – when the Daleks formed their alliance with various other races and the traitorous Guardian of the Solar System, Mavic Chen – the efficient saucer design had been adopted by various other races. This is evident from the images of the Dalek base on Kembel provided by Space Special Security agents Marc Cory and Bret Vyon before their deaths.

It was from Kembel that the Daleks planned to operate their Time Destructor, and from their base that Dalek Pursuit Ships were sent after the Doctor when he and his friends stole a vital component and escaped in Mavic Chen's own ship – a Spar 740.

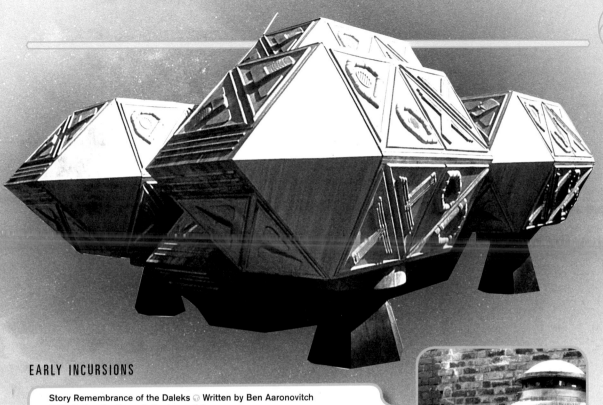

EARLY INCURSIONS

Story Remembrance of the Daleks ⊙ Written by Ben Aaronovitch
⊙ Featuring the Seventh Doctor and Ace
⊙ First broadcast 5–26 October 1988 ⊙ 4 episodes

With advanced Time Corridor and Temporal Shift technology, the Daleks rarely needed to land on Earth in force, except for a full-scale invasion. For incursions and surveillance, they preferred to remain undetected.

An exception was the Shoreditch Incident, when a shielded Imperial Dalek Mothership despatched an attack squad and Special Weapons Dalek to London in 1963 using a small shuttle craft.

Although it could not be detected on RADAR, there is no doubt that the arrival and departure of the shuttle was witnessed by many bemused Londoners. The shuttle and the Mothership were destroyed by the so-called Hand of Omega, a remote stellar manipulator that had been reprogrammed by the Doctor.

INVASION FORCE

Story The Dalek Invasion of Earth ⊙ Written by Terry Nation
⊙ Featuring the First Doctor, Susan, Barbara and Ian
⊙ First broadcast 21 November–26 December 1964 ⊙ 6 episodes

It was the standard saucer-shaped craft that the Daleks deployed in their invasion of Earth in the twenty-second century. There are conflicting reports about the exact design of the main Dalek saucers used by Dalek Earth Force. Originally they were thought to be a cumbersome, rather squat shape. But more recent documentation shows craft very similar to those that later attacked the Game Station (see p.88). The saucers were destroyed in the eruptions caused when the Doctor and his friends set off a powerful explosive capsule in Dalek mine workings.

BATTLE CRUISER DESIGN

> Story Resurrection of the Daleks ⊙ Written by Eric Saward
> ⊙ Featuring the Fifth Doctor, Tegan and Turlough
> ⊙ First broadcast 8–15 February 1984 ⊙ 2 episodes

The classic Dalek saucer went through various changes as Dalek technology improved and the design developed. The Battle Cruiser that survived the Dalek-Movellan war and went in search of Davros was a basic saucer design with additional storage and weapons system areas added.

The Battle Cruiser deployed awesome firepower against the spacestation prison where Earth was holding the Daleks' creator, Davros, in suspended animation

after his capture and trial. The Cruiser easily destroyed the station's complement of fighters and disabled the defences. The Cruiser then docked to allow a Dalek force augmented by brainwashed duplicate humans to take control of the station and release Davros.

A separate mission via a time corridor to Earth in the 1980s recovered stored canisters of a deadly virus the Movellans had used against the Daleks, and for which they wanted Davros to develop a cure. It also drew the Doctor's TARDIS to the same point – part of a Dalek plan to infiltrate Gallifrey and assassinate the Time Lord High Council. The plan was thwarted when both Davros and the Doctor released the Movellan virus and the Dalek Battle Cruiser was destroyed when the spacestation's self-destruct was activated.

TRANQUIL REPOSE

Story Revelation of the Daleks ☺ Written by Eric Saward
☺ Featuring the Sixth Doctor and Peri
☺ First broadcast 23–30 March 1985 ☺ 2 episodes

Davros escaped the destruction of his prison, and made his way to the planet Necros, where he claimed to be the 'Great Healer' and took control of the cemetery and cryogenic facility called Tranquil Repose. Funded by an unscrupulous corporation, Davros set about processing the dead and near-dead as food. He used the profits to create a new race of Daleks, genetically modifying cryogenically suspended humans to become Dalek creatures. Staff from Tranquil Repose contacted Skaro, and the Supreme Dalek sent a taskforce to capture Davros. The Skaro Daleks defeated Davros's new force, and he was taken back to Skaro in a specially modified Prison Saucer to stand trial for his crimes against the Dalek race.

DALEK ARMY

Story Planet of the Daleks ☺ Written by Terry Nation
☺ Featuring the Third Doctor and Jo
☺ First broadcast 7 April–12 May 1973 ☺ 6 episodes

A group of Thals sent to the planet Spiridon had discovered the Daleks were experimenting on the native Spiridons to learn their secrets of invisibility. Expecting to encounter a small scientific force, the Thals learned that there were actually ten thousand Daleks on Spiridon, most held in suspended animation in huge underground caverns.

Arriving on Spiridon in its distinctive two-tier Command Saucer, the Dalek Supreme ordered huge Dalek Space Transporters to be made ready for the vast army to embark. But the Doctor and the Thals were able to ensure the army stayed frozen. Although the Dalek Supreme and its command squad survived, the Thals stole the Command Saucer and returned to Skaro.

THE EXXILON EXPEDITION

Story Death to the Daleks ☺ Written by Terry Nation
☺ Featuring the Third Doctor and Sarah
☺ First broadcast 23 February–16 March 1974 ☺ 4 episodes

During a hiatus between the Dalek Wars, the Earth Marine Space Corps discovered that the planet Exxilon was rich in the rare mineral Parrinium – the only cure for the great space plague. But as soon as the MSC ship arrived on Exxilon it lost all power, as did a small Dalek saucer. The Daleks themselves were not completely affected, but they lost the use of their standard weapons, and replaced their blasters with machine-gun attachments. The humans and Daleks formed an uneasy alliance to mine Parrinium, and found that the ancient City of the Exxilons was responsible for the power losses. The Daleks destroyed the collecting beacon and the Doctor disrupted the City's computer system, restoring power to the ships.

DALEK INVASION FLEET

The Game Station and planet Earth itself were attacked by a Dalek fleet made up of some 200 ships. Classic Dalek saucers, each ship could carry an army of 2,000 Daleks, ready to disembark and form an attack force at any time.

Like all their craft, the Dalek saucers were powered by vast, incredibly powerful anti-gravity engines that spun them through space at great speed. Equipped with advanced camouflage systems, they could hide from detection using a transmitted signal that used wave cancellation to mask their presence.

The fleet was ultimately destroyed by Rose Tyler. Saturated with temporal energy from the Time Vortex itself, which she absorbed through the TARDIS, she dispersed the fleet, turning the Daleks to dust…

The interior of the typical Dalek saucer was divided into many separate levels, with a central shaft running down the middle. As well as standard service elevators, Daleks could use their levitation abilities to move between floors.

The Emperor's flagship also contained compartments where kidnapped humans were kept until they were needed for conversion into Dalek genetic material. The vast

Story
Bad Wolf & The Parting of the Ways
Written by
Russell T Davies
Featuring
the Ninth Doctor, Rose and Captain Jack
First broadcast
11–18 June 2005
2 episodes

INSPIRED DESIGN

These Dalek ships were the most impressive Dalek craft to be realised in **Doctor Who** so far. The detailed computer-generated images created by The Mill were based on designs from the Art Department. These designs were themselves inspired by the Dalek saucers in the classic comic-strip stories that had appeared in annuals and the magazine *TV Century 21* in the mid 1960s. These distinctive designs included saucers, transolar discs, the massive Dalek city on Skaro and even the large-domed Dalek Emperor himself.

and impressive Dalek Emperor itself was housed in the central area of the flagship.

Like individual Daleks, the ships were protected by force fields and armed with impressive weaponry, including missiles which homed in on their prey using a thronic aura beam, and could explode with more power than an erupting volcano.

As well as the post-Time War assault on Earth, Dalek saucers have been reported in battle against the robot Mechonoids, and in operations centred on the planets Solturis, Phryne and Amaryll, amongst others.

Above: Paintings and drawings of the exterior and inside of the massive Dalek saucers.

VOID SHIP

Towards the end of the Great Time War, the Daleks realised that they could not defeat the Time Lords without being totally destroyed themselves. So the Cult of Skaro – an elite group of four Daleks charged by the Dalek Emperor with devising strategies to win the War – devised a new type of craft – a Void Ship. This spherical craft could travel through the space between universes. Here the Daleks hid and waited for the War to end.

When the Great Time War was over, the Void Ship appeared in our world. The Cult of Skaro emerged – bringing with them the Genesis Ark. They hoped that this stolen Time Lord device would provide the means of rebuilding the Dalek race. It was in fact a dimensionally transcendental prison – containing thousands, perhaps millions, of captured Daleks, ready to escape and conquer.

Story
Army of Ghosts & Doomsday
Written by
Russell T Davies
Featuring
the Tenth Doctor, Rose and Mickey
First broadcast
1–8 July 2006
2 episodes

SONTARAN SHIPS

The Sontarans are a brutal race of warriors dedicated to warfare. They have been at war with their sworn enemies the Rutans for thousands of years. The Sontarans come from a high-gravity planet and reproduce by cloning in vast numbers on designated clone worlds. They are all identical in appearance.

Sontaran ships conform to a few standard designs. Most common is the distinctive spherical Scout Ship, also used for clandestine operations as they are small enough to avoid Rutan — and other — detection systems. Some more advanced Scout Ships can be placed in 'clear' when they have landed — making them invisible.

FORCED LANDING

Story The Time Warrior ☺ Written by Robert Holmes
☺ Featuring the Third Doctor, Sarah and UNIT
☺ First broadcast 15 December 1973–5 January 1974 ☺ 4 episodes

The first known incidence of a Sontaran Scout Ship landing on Earth was in medieval times. Commander Jingo Linx of the Fifth Sontaran Army Space Fleet was on a reconnaissance mission when his ship was attacked by a squadron of Rutan fighters and forced down on Earth. It was damaged in the crash, so Linx used an osmic projector to time jump into the future and kidnap scientists from the twentieth century who could help repair the Sontaran craft.

ASSESSMENT SURVEY

Story The Sontaran Experiment ☺ Written by Bob Baker and Dave Martin
☺ Featuring the Fourth Doctor, Sarah and Harry
☺ First broadcast 22 February–1 March 1975 ☺ 2 episodes

The basic design of the Scout Ship had changed little by the time Field Major Styre of the Sontaran G3 Military Assessment Survey set up a secret base on the abandoned future Earth. Styre's mission was to determine whether humans were strong enough to withstand a Sontaran attack. But he was killed after engaging in single combat with the Doctor and the attack was called off when he failed to report to his fleet.

ASSAULT SHIP

Story The Invasion of Time ☻ Written by David Agnew
☻ Featuring the Fourth Doctor, Leela and K-9
☻ First broadcast 4 February–11 March 1978 ☻ 6 episodes

A Warship spearheaded the Sontaran attack on Gallifrey, following up
an infiltration by the Sontarans' temporary allies the Vardans. A group of
the elite Sontaran Special Space Service led by Commander Stor osmic-
projected into the very heart of the Capitol of Gallifrey – the Panopticon,
meeting place of the High Council of Time Lords. The Sontaran main fleet
waited in standard arrow formation for Stor and his unit to secure Gallifrey.

But Stor was killed, and his unit destroyed when the Time Lord who had
pretended to be working with them led the Time Lord resistance against
the Sontarans. That Time Lord was the recently invested Lord President,
otherwise known as the Doctor.

BATTLE GROUP

Story The Two Doctors ☻ Written by Robert Holmes
☻ Featuring the Sixth Doctor and Peri & the Second Doctor and Jamie
☻ First broadcast 16 February–2 March 1985 ☻ 3 episodes

A planned Earth landing, albeit clandestine,
was made by Group Marshal Stike. This
followed his Ninth Sontaran Battle Group's
successful attack on the research space
station *Camera* and his capture of the
Second Doctor.

Taking over a Spanish villa on Earth,
Stike and his accomplices hoped to isolate
the Doctor's symbiotic nuclei and with it
perfect their time-travel technology. The Sixth
Doctor was able to intervene and save his
past self.

Story
The Sontaran Stratagem
& The Poison Sky
Written by Helen Raynor
Featuring
the Tenth Doctor, Donna,
Martha and UNIT
First broadcast
26 April–3 May 2008
2 episodes

SONTARAN WARSHIPS

Far more powerful and well-equipped than the Scout Ship is the Sontaran Warship. Again, most conform to one of a few standard designs. Huge, majestic, and lethal, Sontaran Warships are armed with a variety of weapons, including enough missiles to destroy entire planets. They go into battle in a distinctive arrow-shaped formation. The ship commanded by General Staal of the Tenth Sontaran Battle Fleet carried a full battle group, including Staal's adjutant Commander Skorr – also known as Skorr the Bloodbringer – and the ship's operations officer Lieutenant Skree.

   In orbit high above the Earth, the ship remained undetected while Staal's stratagem to turn the Earth into a Sontaran Clone World moved forward. Despite replacing UNIT soldiers and the Doctor's friend Martha Jones with cloned copies, Staal was unable to stop the Doctor discovering his plans.

PREPARING FOR WAR

Whereas the Sontaran ship that was seen over Gallifrey in *The Invasion of Time* was a physical miniature model, the Warship in *The Sontaran Stratagem* was a computer-generated image created by effects house The Mill.

The images on these pages show some initial designs as well as the final, impressive Scout Ship 'Pod' – completely realistic and ready for action.

THE TARDIS

Of all the starships and spacestations the Doctor has found in his travels, the strangest surely is his own TARDIS. While the Time Lords shunned conventional space travel after they discovered the secrets of space-time travel, the TARDIS is, amongst other things, essentially a spaceship.

The Doctor's TARDIS is actually a Type 40 TT Capsule. Transcendentally engineered to be bigger inside than outside, the small exterior hides a huge control room and many other chambers. But the TARDIS is old and, by Time Lord standards, far from the latest model.

The TARDIS is fitted with a Chameleon Circuit, which means it can change its outward appearance to blend in with its surroundings when it lands. But – like many other TARDIS components – the circuit is broken. It failed while the Doctor was visiting Earth in the 1960s, so the TARDIS remains stuck in the shape it adopted to blend into that time and place – a London police box.

Before they were destroyed in the Great Time War, the Time Lords had built giant citadels and mighty spacestations. But their most impressive achievement will always be their TARDIS time ships.